POOR
BLOODY
INFANTRY

Other books by Bernard Martin

STRANGE VIGOUR
a biography of Sun Yat-sen

OUR CHIEF OF MEN
a short biography of Oliver Cromwell

THE ANCIENT MARINER AND THE
AUTHENTIC NARRATIVE

JOHN NEWTON
a biography

JOHN NEWTON AND THE SLAVE TRADE

with Mark Spurrell

THE JOURNAL OF A SLAVE TRADER
John Newton 1750–1754

with Shui Chien-tung

MAKERS OF CHINA
Confucius to Mao

for young readers

THE PAGODA PLOT
adventure in Burma

RED TREASURE
a novel

THE WALKABOUT PLOT
adventure in Australia

POOR
BLOODY
INFANTRY

A Subaltern on the Western Front 1916-1917

Bernard Martin

JOHN MURRAY

© Bernard Martin 1987

First published 1987
by John Murray (Publishers) Ltd
50 Albemarle Street, London W1X 4BD

Typeset by Inforum Ltd, Portsmouth
Printed and bound in Great Britain by
The Bath Press, Avon

British Library CIP data

Martin, Bernard
    Poor bloody infantry : a subaltern on
    the Western Front 1916–1917.
    1. World War, 1914–1918——Campaigns——
    Western   2. World War, 1914–1918——
    Personal narratives, British
    I. Title
    940.4'144'0924   D544

    ISBN 0–7195–4374–6

For
ROSALIND

Contents

Illustrations

Photographs 1–5, 11, 13 and 14 are the Author's.
The rest are by courtesy of the Imperial War Museum.

A Fragment of Memory

In 1916, after six months in trenches, I had eight days' leave at home in Scotland. On my way back for another dose of war, I chanced to hear the opening words of a recruiting song, intended to shame young men into volunteering for military service, *When you sit by the fire in an old man's chair, and your neighbours talk of the war, will you say, I was not with the Forces then* . . . I didn't listen to more, the song didn't apply to me; my thoughts were already ahead with my regiment in France, wondering what casualties they would have suffered while I was on leave. But when I landed at Boulogne and was swapping yarns about leave with a chap I knew whom I met in the Hotel de Paris, my memory suddenly disgorged that opening phrase, *When you sit by the fire in an old man's chair.* I was amazed: as though I had missed the point of a funny story and woken up in the night laughing. The life of an infantry subaltern in the trenches was calculated in weeks (in 1916, the average was three weeks). As someone aptly wrote, 'Subalterns do not last long.' The fact that it was impossible to imagine such a distant future, such a stretching of life, left the unconsidered thought sticking out after I'd parted from my friend, fading only gradually as I walked the last few kilometres of my journey to rejoin my regiment at a derelict coal-mining village with the grand but improbable name of Philosophe.

Well, the Old Man's Chair has happened. In 1983, a few days before my eighty-sixth birthday, I completed my last regular job of work. I was asked by a University Extra-Mural

1

Board to make a tape-recording of my experiences in the Great War. I'd written a dozen books on various subjects, never about war. It was explained that my stint of trench warfare had been exceptionally long, that there can be few still living who took an active part in going 'over the top' in such famous battles as the Somme and Passchendaele. So I made the tape as from an old man's chair, and here offer an extended version as a fragment of autobiography.* Perhaps, as justification for so personal an account, I may be allowed to echo the words of Isaac Walton, the Compleat Angler, 'the reader will not credit that such things could be, but I was there, and I saw it.'

---

* The tape was published in June 1985, entitled *One Man's War 1914–1918*. Available from Sussex Tapes, Townsend, Poulshot, Devizes, Wilts, SN10 1SD.

CHAPTER ONE

The Unexpected

Did anyone in Britain expect war in 1914? Boys didn't. We were taught history, all about wars, rebellions and revolutions: the good old days – good because exciting. Britain's heroes were fighting men, who defeated Spain and Holland and France, who satisfactorily splashed the map of the world with the red of our Empire. We were not entirely ignorant of political affairs – centuries of wars with France ended by the *Entente Cordiale*; Germany the only possible enemy in the twentieth century, and Winston Churchill (our bright young First Lord of the Admiralty) boasting openly of Britain's deterrent – the Royal Navy. Our Dreadnoughts outclassed the Kaiser's ships. Every upper-class and middle-class schoolboy in England knew the names and gun-sizes of the great battleships of both fleets. Germany would not dare to start a war while Britain so definitely ruled the waves.

The unexpected happened. We could hardly believe our fortune. Adults preached that war is morally wrong, some had been saying so for years, but this war was different, even pacifists could see that: a just war, forced on us by the German attack on Belgium, by Germany breaking sacred treaties; a righteous war, a great and glorious adventure, patriotic and God on our side too.

All the boys I knew longed to be involved but politicians, newspapers, our parents and masters expected the war to be over by Christmas: and volunteers for the new Kitchener's Army had to be over nineteen. I was seventeen years and three

3

months old, still at school. Bliss was it in that dawn to be alive, but to be too young was very hell.

Rumours galore – spies everywhere, Russian soldiers come to support what the Kaiser called, 'England's contemptible little army'. I spent a whole day at a level-crossing on the main line of the North British Railway hoping to see a southbound train with all the blinds down to conceal Russians, but my luck was out. However, I soon saw a real act of war, the sinking of HMS *Pathfinder* by a German submarine. I was on holiday with my family in Berwickshire, and several times watched this cruiser from the high cliffs of St Abb's Head patrolling about the approaches to the Firth of Forth. I didn't exactly *see* her sink. I switched my field-glasses from the warship to fishing boats and other vessels: when I looked again HMS *Pathfinder* was gone. The St Abb's lifeboat picked up a few survivors. I looked in vain for an official announcement of this loss in the newspapers. It wasn't a rumour. I was there, and as good as saw it. War became a reality.

My elder brother wrote from London saying he had enlisted in The Artists' Rifles. A week later he sent a newspaper with a picture of himself and other Artists' Rifles digging a trench in a London park. The war was coming near, our family involved. Soon my turn came. The War Office ordered that smallarms everywhere must be under guard, night and day, in case of invasion. My school cadet corps had an armoury in an attic, containing three Lee Enfield rifles (used one day every year when the army made a range available to us) and 200 obsolete cavalry carbines, for which no ammunition had been made since the South African war. A letter from the CO of the cadet corps ordered me to report for guard duty at the armoury. I couldn't have been more thrilled if the order had come direct to me from Kitchener: it was grand to march through the streets of Edinburgh in cadet uniform and sit all night with another cadet in the stuffy attic guarding our weapons: but no one believed an invasion likely, and I got stuck several nights with a chap I didn't much like.

At home we supposed the Artists' Rifles were Territorials, for service only in England. It came as a surprise when, before Christmas, my brother was sent on active service to France. In childhood there had never been envy between my brother and me; our temperaments were different, we seldom clamoured for the same things, or competed for schoolboy fame. Now I *was* envious: he, my brother, actually fighting in the greatest war in the history of man, and I too young even to be accepted as a recruit in Kitchener's new army. Not fair! I told myself, with a child's faith in equality and justice. Not fair he should have this sudden leap to the very peak of ambition, just because he came into the world a bit before me. Not his fault, of course, but I envied him. Neither he nor I had chosen when to be born, we hadn't even chosen our parents, or our nationality: we might have been heathen Chinese, or Hottentots, or – let's face the extreme – Germans. He and I could have grown up with silly names like Karl, or Hans, or Bruno!

I find it hard now to believe I could have been so stupid at the age of seventeen. When envy gave way to disappointment an idea came into my mind, one of those unsought inspirations which arrive complete, from goodness knows where. I knew girls, not a day older than me, already taking lessons in first-aid, training to be VAD nurses; surely there must be similar non-combatant work for men at that age? Of course; stretcher-bearers. In a flash I saw myself on a battlefield, carrying wounded men to safety, shells bursting around us. I cut school one morning and dodged off to a recruiting-centre. The sergeant gave me the up-and-down stare which I later discovered was the hallmark of NCOs.

'What's your age, sonny?'

'Seventeen and three quarters, sergeant.'

He laughed, so I added hastily. 'I've not come to volunteer as a combatant. I know I'm too young. I want to be a stretcher-bearer.'

Another up-and-down stare, another laugh. To my surprise he turned from me to a private soldier sitting at a table. 'Get off that chair,' he ordered, 'lie down on the floor, on your back.' When the man was prostrate the sergeant turned to me and said mildly, 'Pick him up . . . he's wounded . . . carry him out through the door to Casualty clearing.' I hesitated. 'Go on . . . he'll bleed to death if you don't get him to a dressing station quickly.' After a pause he added, 'What are you waiting for? He's only medium weight, about eleven or twelve stone I guess.' The lesson was clear. Age didn't matter for stretcher-bearers. But they needed fully developed muscles. He kicked the boot of the private. 'Get up . . . you ain't got to die of wounds . . . not yet . . . reckon you've been saved.'

Despondently I said, 'I understand, sergeant.'

'Seventeen and three quarters,' he murmured reflectively, as though the fraction made it a fairy story. 'Never mind, sonny. Pity there ain't more with your pluck. Your time will come. No one is going to stop you getting older – happens to everyone, no one's discovered yet how to stop you doing that.'

I had to tell someone. Soon the story of how I'd made a fool of myself was school gossip. The headmaster sent for me. Against one wall of his study the school Roll of Honour was propped, removed temporarily from Assembly Hall for the addition of more names, and for an asterisk to be added to my brother's name, indicating that he was on active service. 'A record any school could be proud of', the Head said: and then calmly, as though announcing some trivial school rule, he gave me information which changed my life.

'You, and some of your friends, will be interested in a War

Office pronouncement I've just received. The Regular Army has a Special Reserve of Officers; something to do with filling unexpected vacancies in the Indian Army. You can imagine an officer taken ill out there, obliged to return home, leaving a rather urgent vacancy for a white officer to command native soldiers. Applications for commissions in this reserve are now invited from school cadet corps members. It's not like Kitchener Army volunteers, serving for the duration. These Special Reserve commissions are permanent. You have all got your life professions planned but you need not worry about after the war. This war is to end war, as the politicians promise; anyway, whatever army remains afterwards will be only a kind of police force, with two or three weeks service a year, like the Territorials. You intend to be a doctor, read Medicine at the University here. I'm sure that will still be possible after the war is won.' He picked up a paper from his desk. 'Applicants must be recommended by someone of good standing who has known the applicant personally for at least three years. The age limit is eighteen.'

'Nineteen, sir,' I murmured in polite correction.

'Nineteen for Kitchener's Army,' he explained. 'The Special Reserve for Officers is eighteen. It's quite clear on the application form.' He read aloud, 'Applicants must be not less than eighteen years of age.' Was I dreaming? Could this be true? Some mistake surely?

'Surprised me too,' the Head said. 'Think about it. Take the form, show it to your father. If you decide to apply, and have his consent, I'll send your application to the War Office.'

So a miracle came to pass. On the 25th April 1915, one day after my eighteenth birthday, I was gazetted a Second-Lieutenant in the reserve battalion of the 64th Regiment of Foot in the regular army, an infantry regiment which boasted a long list of battle honours – the Crimea, the

Indian Mutiny, Ashanti, Zulu wars and others.

Everyone in England was class-conscious, born into a social class and remaining in it for life. My family was middle class. We lived in London till I was fourteen, then moved to Edinburgh where class was less marked, '*A man's a man for a' that*', education being the only sensible distinction between one man and another. In 1914 many young men of our class, nineteen years old or older, enlisted as private soldiers, as did my brother, choosing an élite unit like The Artists' Rifles, where they served with friends of their own class.

'Fifty pounds to spend on uniform!' exclaimed my elder sister when I proudly held up the cheque sent by the War Office. 'Crumbs! Fifty pounds will buy you enough clothes to last a lifetime.' A lifetime – *my* lifetime; perhaps she's right, maybe the uniform will last longer than me. Do they collect the uniforms from officers killed in action, I wondered? Is there a second-hand market for dead men's uniforms? The military tailor crossed off several items on the War Office list. 'You won't need this, sir, that's obsolete, not been in stock these ten years . . . wait till you get to the Front before spending money on a canteen, sir, roads in Flanders littered with thrown away canteens . . . this regulation great coat – heavy material, double breasted, ankle length – exhausting to march a mile in it; unless you expect to fight Germans round the North Pole! Let me make you one of the short British Warms instead, sir, not regulation, but customers tell me they're more practical in trenches.' Such cavalier treatment of a War Office instruction worried me faintly, but all life was a dream. When the uniform arrived I accepted the homage of parents and sisters, but hardly dared to go out. I looked both ways along the road to make sure no soldiers were near, and when I'd gone a few hundred yards and spotted a man in uniform coming towards me I turned back to the sanctuary of home rather than face his salute.

Next evening I began the longest journey I'd ever made: a night train to London, another train to Southampton, an all-night voyage in a small ship in a rough sea to the Channel Islands. On that long journey, I reminded myself for encouragement that I was taking a five-hundred-mile step in the direction of my Mecca – the place where war was being fought.

The reserve battalion of my regiment, generally known as North Staffordshire Regiment, occupied a fortress, built to defy Napoleon. The Adjutant, severe as any schoolmaster, pointed across the citadel – 'Officers' Mess over there, Mr Martin. Wait in the ante-room till a batman is ready to show you your quarters.' I sat in the ante-room looking at magazines, as one does at the dentist's. A lieutenant entered and walked up to me briskly. 'I'm the senior subaltern here,' he said in an official manner. 'It's my job to instruct you in Mess customs.' He enumerated a daunting number of do's and don'ts – avoid certain chairs reserved for senior officers, be last going in to dinner, strict observance of traditional rituals on Guest Nights (Fridays, whether any guests or not), never rise from table before the President of Mess, and so on and so on. He concluded, 'I shall keep an eye on you and tell you when you go wrong, but no one else will speak to you for a fortnight, that's tradition. After the fortnight you'll find we're quite a friendly lot.'

Sent to Coventry – a punishment imposed by boys on one of their number guilty of anti-social behaviour; ignored by companions as though one didn't exist . . . spoken to by no one. Here, in the army, in an Officers' Mess, I was sent to Coventry – fourteen days without the option and, as in Wonderland, sentence before crime. I had done nothing anti-social, not even committed a faux-pas.

For me the loneliness of that first fortnight was severe. I had never been lonely at school. Now, five hundred miles from anyone I knew, only myself to talk to, me and my thoughts! I tried to persuade myself it wasn't altogether a bad thing, to argue with my own thoughts instead of with other people, to carry discussions to conclusions.

I took immediate comfort in reading over and over again my Commission, with its seal of His Majesty King George:

> To Our Trusty and Well-beloved Bernard Davis Martin Greeting. We reposing especial Trust and Confidence in your Loyalty, Courage and good Conduct do by these Presents Appoint you to be an Officer in Our Special Reserve of Officers . . . at all times to exercise and well discipline the inferior Officers and Men serving under you . . . and do hereby Command them to Obey you . . .

What did Mess customs matter? Why worry about this Coventry custom, or what other officers might think of me? I was proud of my commission, my personal relationship with the King of the greatest empire on earth, but during my fortnight of self-examination I wondered what it was going to be like living amongst men; would they look down on me as coming straight from school? I must avoid showing too much enthusiasm for athletics and sports' records, keep my mouth shut till I knew what other subjects men talk about. For several generations my family had been Nonconformists and consequently rather despised by conformers, but in Scotland the state Kirk (Presbyterian) was tolerant, cooperating with all Protestants. I soon learned that in the army anything but Church of England was called 'Fancy religion'. It would be prudent to keep off the subject.

After Coventry I was thankful to have smiles and some

friendly comments, but I was amongst professionals with a military outlook on life, orthodox and conforming to established customs. I was worried a little because nothing happened about my training. However, before long the battalion received a number of new subalterns and at once we began parades.

Army discipline was no trouble; fundamentally the same as at school, accepting the authority of those appointed as superiors, at school the masters, in the army all of higher rank. I took with me into the army a willingness to conform, and a keen enthusiasm to learn which made even elementary squad drill and the more complex company drill a pleasure. I enjoyed open-air life, sleeping in a tent on a cliff high above the sea, early morning runs on footpaths round the island's bays and route-marches through country lanes. It was spring-time for me, days filled with abundant life, no drudgery, no dreary tasks, always the assurance that ahead lay my heart's desire when training would end and I should lead men in a righteous cause.

To be sure, keenness was a little blunted by constant repetition of routine drills, just occasionally we asked one another if there were not aspects of war transcending drill which we ought to learn. Bayonet Fighting and Musketry were obvious examples. As though in answer to our thought a Colour-Sergeant from an Irish regiment turned up to instruct us in the finer points of Bayonet Fighting. An assault course was made in a disused moat round the citadel of the fort. We took turns charging down the course prodding life-sized dummies stuffed with straw, some erect, some prone.

Now sir, start with your balance controlled . . . feet well apart . . . rifle gripped firm, like as you cuddle a girl . . . Mother o' God, tisn't a sack o' straw, 'tis a bloody Hun . . .

don't saunter up as you might to a wench you're courting. *In . . . out . . . on to the next*, keep those words singing in your head . . . *In* – all your weight behind it, sir. *Out* – right foot in his belly and sharp tug. No fear o' hurting him, he's already dead or nigh dead. *On to the next*, all the way to Berlin, sir . . . Saints in Heaven, if you stop to wonder what next he'll have his bayonet in your guts. It's him or you. Like with a girl who dithers – you don't take no for an answer . . . And, sir, for the love o' Saint Michael, remember to yell. Jungle beasts roar to paralyse their prey . . . never fear to burst your lungs wi' an almighty yell, give a yell after every Hun you stick . . . and remember *on to the next*.

Bayonet practice was a game, a competitive game, and I was good at it. Once, when the Commanding Officer and the Adjutant came to see what we were up to, the Irishman picked on me to demonstrate. I became an actor with an audience, conscious when I stabbed a mock enemy or tugged my weapon clear from a bloodless corpse that everyone was watching, including the instructor and Commanding Officer; all judging if my movements were swift and sure. And when I stood breathless before the audience I was pleased with myself and tucked away in my mind the Adjutant's observation, 'Good show'. A game, an active game, splendid exercise; but a bit remote from reality because officers are never armed with bayonets. When we go into action we fight with pistols.

I was lucky to be chosen for a course on musketry at Hayling Island, a strenuous course lasting several weeks, the instructors regular army experts. Musketry is fundamental for infantry soldiers, including as it does practical subjects like map-reading, judging distances, and fire-direction: for me excitingly imaginative.

I qualified as a First Class Instructor, and returned to

Guernsey pleased with myself. But the majesty of my success wasn't apparent until the Regimental-Sergeant-Major accosted me. This formidable Warrant Officer halted with a click of the heels which seemed to say, when an RSM comes to a halt all the rest of Nature stands still. I did anyway. After an impressive pause his right hand swept upwards in a superb salute. I was overwhelmed. I did not dare to return such a gesture, just stood awkwardly, my head bowed in reverence. 'Sir, I see from Battalion Orders you did very well at the School of Musketry, bringing honour to the Regiment. As the senior Warrant Officer may I express our congratulations, sir.' I was very embarrassed, couldn't even say, 'Thank you, Sergeant-Major'. After a moment of silent dignity he stepped back four paces, saluted again and uttered the one word 'Sir', before doing an about-turn and marching away.

I supposed my qualification in musketry would be made use of but batches of men were sent overseas and not replaced by recruits. Our training became spasmodic and perfunctory. Occasionally we did an all-day march round the coast roads of the island, or were taken by senior officers to one of the many derelict Martello Towers and shown how the place should be defended or attacked – excursions usually ending in disagreements amongst our instructors.

I shared a tent with a man old enough to be my father, a nice chap who treated me as a companion, overlooking my teenage. We used to 'make ourselves scarce' (an art in army life at which I became very proficient), and slip away to the billiards room of the Officers' Mess where he instructed me in that high-class game. I can recall his laugh, 'Good pot, old man, but don't overdo it, not too big a break, remember the saying – good at billiards reveals a mis-spent youth.' I told him he had an unfair advantage because his name was Potter. After we'd been together some months, Potter told me a friend of his was coming to stay in St Peter's Port, a woman friend. In carefully chosen words (not wanting to disturb my innocence) he said, 'Don't worry if I'm not in the tent when you wake in the morning.' I only half realised the situation, but felt it was something about which I ought to be shocked. Potter was a kind and gentle man who influenced me more than I knew. We shared a tent for six months before I was transferred to Sark and then to Alderney. We never met again. During the Battle of the Somme I wrote in my diary, 'Potter killed'. I never heard any details.

One morning the Adjutant sent for me. 'You are to instruct a class of officers in Musketry, a three-week course . . . mornings nine o'clock to twelve, afternoons fifteen hours to seventeen . . . start today at fifteen hours . . . let me know how it goes.'

The class consisted of twenty brother officers, all junior to me in rank by a few days, some a lot older in years. I was terrified, rushed to my notebooks, fortunately so detailed that as I read I could hear the voice of the instructor. I began with the elementary lesson which started the Hayling Island course, 'I am going to show you how to fire your rifle in the standing position: what I mean by THAT is THIS,' (followed by a demonstration). To my consternation the class roared with laughter. At Hayling Island I hadn't thought this wording funny. Now my class showed me it was: indeed so funny that it became a *bon mot* for the rest of the course. When I asked a question, the reply, as like as not, would be prefaced with, 'What THAT means is THIS . . .' Not very subtle, perhaps, but good-natured fun amongst friends, and the class let me see they were impressed by my general performance. This course was important for me. It taught me how to speak to an audience and I felt I was no longer only an officer-recruit, a learner. I was making a contribution in the war effort.

Like everyone in Britain we depended for news from the

Front on official reports. Pictures and photographs of trenches may have existed in 1915. None came my way. Occasionally wounded officers from hospital turned up at our Mess, usually awaiting orders to join the second battalion in India. Naturally we asked, 'What's it like at the Front?' Always the same reply, 'Hell. And you fellows who want to get there are barmy. A week in the trenches and you'll do any damned wangle to escape.' Which was no answer. Maybe; we told one another, maybe these chaps have done their bit and are off to cushy jobs. They don't want to talk . . . But think what we should feel after the war, living alongside men who had *seen* war, *heard* war, *felt* war, if we had only learned the damned drills!

So we continued to march hither and thither, to and fro, and repeat drills without even a distant glimpse of what we longed to experience at close range. Indeed, some of us grumbled openly, even questioning how much of what we were taught could be necessary in trench warfare.

One day, to our surprise and delight, two packing cases turned up, from goodness knows where, labelled *Selection of Hand-Grenades*. We opened the cases on the large field used as a parade ground, opposite the Married Quarters. Instructions explained how each type of grenade worked, how to insert detonators, the safety catch or pin to be released before the bomb was thrown, and the number of seconds, after throwing, before the explosion.

'Bags I try the first,' claimed a rather assertive chap. We stood around in a group, counting the seconds. The explosion, a lot louder than anyone expected, was followed by . . . zip . . . zip . . . zip, fragments of metal whizzing past.

'Damned dangerous things!'

'Not intended for use in open battle, they're for trenches, to throw *from* a trench at an approaching enemy.'

The chap who had taken upon himself authority, pointed

across the field and said, 'There's a ditch over there like a trench, this side of Married Quarters. Let's take turns, each of us throwing from the ditch while the rest stand well away.'

So we did – at first one at a time, then four or five in the trench all throwing together and ducking until after the explosions. It was exciting, realistic, war in kid gloves, so to say.

That night was Guest Night, with traditional protocol; a toast to the King, the band playing the National Anthem, a toast to the Prince of Wales (the Colonel-in-Chief of our regiment) the band playing 'God Bless the Prince of Wales'. At last the President of Mess rose to announce, 'Gentlemen, you may smoke.' The Mess Sergeant, dignified and self-important as any diplomat, started his usual circumnavigation of the long table carrying two boxes of Havana cigars, holding them before each diner in turn, honouring a tradition, since few subalterns could afford such expensive smokes. Another five minutes and the President would rise again, pause for the Colonel and Adjutant and any guest to do likewise, and then lead the way to the anteroom door. That would be the welcome signal that we were free at last to 'get down' as children say. When the Mess Sergeant was only a third of the way round the table, a kitchen-orderly hastened to his side, and whispered something, evidently important. At once the Sergeant marched to the head of the table and spoke to the President in a low voice. The President seemed confused, then whispered to the Colonel and to the Adjutant. All three rose and left the room. Something was wrong. None of us moved. The Sergeant remained standing in silence by the vacant chair of the President. What next? The clockwork of routine had run down, and no one knew where the key was kept.

At last with immense reluctance the Sergeant shook himself, lifted his head and spoke, 'Gentlemen . . . an accident . . . children from the Married Quarters found an unexploded grenade in the ditch, played catch with it . . . Sergeant Bright's little girl is killed, three others taken to hospital.' After a moment of hesitation he concluded, 'That's all, Gentlemen.'

I went to the funeral: we all did. The Chaplain conducted what was almost a military service; the coffin (such a light one, I thought), carried by the Sergeant-Major and three sergeants, with a guard of honour who reversed arms at the graveside. Instead of the Last Post, the band played *Abide with Me* (only hymn tune they know, I thought). The coroner called it 'death by misadventure', a lawyer's cliché; in truth Madge Bright was a war casualty. I didn't see her die, but it was the first death I had encountered in all my eighteen years. I hadn't even been to a funeral; so this small tragedy made a lasting impression on me.

'A Cook's Tour,' wrote my brother in the first of his letters to give any particulars about his long service in France. The phrase 'Cook's Tour' was in common use for any sight-seeing or tourist journey. How could it apply to a private in The Artists' Rifles on the Western Front? The envelope bore a Censor's stamp, but nothing had been crossed out from a short excited letter, read almost at a glance.

'Just returned from a personally conducted Cook's Tour of the Front, one whole day in a front line trench.' Only a few words more to say he was now back again on the same dull job he'd been doing since his unit came to France on active service – Guard Duty at British Headquarters at Saint Pol, two days' march from the nearest war activity! And my parents and I had supposed that he had been in constant danger for the last eight months.

By the summer of 1915 politicians talked of conscription, which would become necessary when the spate of volunteers dried up. What we did not know was the urgent problem of casualties to infantry subaltern officers: 'they didn't last long'. Some of the early volunteers, still privates in crack units like The Artists' Rifles, were of the social class on which the country depended for commissioned officers.

The daily newspapers published casualty lists, and also extracts from *The London Gazette*. Naturally we looked through these for possible news of friends. One day I saw my brother's name – commissioned a Second-Lieutenant in The Sherwood Foresters. I wrote my congratulations at once. Now he was an officer we could go about together in public if we happened to have leave at the same time. I told him my training in Guernsey seemed to be coming to an end. I should be posted soon to the Western Front. Perhaps we could then wangle a meeting. As I wrote I reminded myself with a little shame that at the start of the war I'd envied my brother his years: childish . . . absurd, and how differently events had transpired. He was still my elder brother but I couldn't refrain from a playful dig, 'We are both officers now, but don't forget army seniority counts from the date of commission, so you will always be my junior!' In practice this wasn't likely to mean much, since we were in different regiments, but I was rather pleased with my little joke, and wondered what he could reply. I addressed my letter to him in France. He never received it. On his third day in the front line he died of wounds. My letter was returned unopened with his personal effects.

The War Office telegram reached my father on a Saturday morning, telling all there was to say, 'died of wounds received in action'. Full stop . . . the end. No more letters from him, no censored news from where he had gone, only recollections of the past to turn over and over and over.

Somehow my father knew I was unprepared. His telegram to me said, 'severely wounded', and two hours later a second telegram, 'died of wounds'. These messages came via the battalion orderly office, so by Saturday evening everyone in the Mess knew. They all showed sympathy in one way or another, but the overwhelming disaster set me apart. My mind became a vacuum, desolated by loneliness. I didn't look back upon the happiness of our family life – loving parents, four children with varied likes and dislikes but dwelling together in harmony – nor did I look forward, imagining ways in which I should surely miss an elder brother.

I had no duties before church parade next morning at the Garrison church in St Peter's Port, a service open to the public. I rather enjoyed the weekly ceremony. We marched into the town, led by the band (as like as not playing inappropriate music, *The girl I left behind me*, or *Who were you with last night*). Officers wore swords, the only occasion when we did; a sword is a childish pleasure, being merely a relic of past military romance, but a sword drawn from the scabbard looks effective and one is always conscious of wearing it. On this occasion the conventional church parade failed to rouse me, nothing in it for a lonely man.

After lunch the Adjutant spoke to me, 'Sorry about your brother; hard on your parents. They'd be glad to see you, I daresay. If you apply for compassionate leave you might get the inside of a week.'

The idea surprised me. I pictured myself undergoing the long journey to Edinburgh, taking home a dismal load of confused thoughts to parents mourning their first-born child. Everything would be out of joint – ship delayed by rough seas, train connections missed, the night *Scotsman* from King's Cross crowded (perhaps not even room to lie down in the corridor), all in contrast to the exciting adventure I felt when I came south.

I took refuge in my tent to be alone, to think. I caught myself glancing now and then across to the half which had been occupied by my friend Potter. He would have given me sensible advice.

Some of the residents in Guernsey had shown us hospitality. Several times I'd been to tea at the home of Mr Champier, the President of the Grower's Association. He lived in a farmhouse amidst fields of flowers grown for export to England. His wife had given me a warm welcome, 'Our children are so young they'll grow up without knowing war. So we shall always be in debt to you brave men; not that we can ever repay such a debt. The least we can do is to make you feel at home whenever you feel like coming. Sunday is the best day for us because even in the busy season we don't work on the Sabbath.'

As the need to talk to someone pressed upon me, I turned to the Champiers. Naturally I shouldn't embarrass them with any mention of my brother's death. I only wanted to feel less lonely. The children were delightful, the girl a year younger than my second sister and two boys just the right age for stories of romantic battles in which a hero fought gallantly, and always won – told by a soldier too: they would listen to any nonsense I made up. They greeted me noisily, demanding the next instalment, or at least a word-by-word repetition of an earlier story. I did my best, but children are ruthless critics – I failed on what Ensign Cutlass did when Napoleon's soldiers attacked Fort George. 'Don't be pests,' said Mrs Champier to her sons, 'You're not to worry him.' To me she said, 'You look tired. One of your late nights playing bridge?' She was teasing, pretending not to approve of the bad habits of subalterns who sat up gambling with cards. I wasn't in the mood for teasing, but my resolution to keep sorrow to myself evaporated in this friendly atmosphere. I answered in a dreary voice which I hardly recognised as mine.

'My brother has died of wounds.'

'Oh *no!*' she protested.

The children stared solemn-faced. I was no longer the cheerful soldier who came to tea on Sundays and told ripping stories of real war. I was now a stranger. For a time I didn't trust myself to speak again. It was years since I'd been so near to weeping (and then only the angry tears of childhood). Mrs Champier began questioning my about my home life, my father's occupation, were my sisters old enough to help my mother with housework and so on. And I responded. I told them how my younger sister impersonated *Alice in Wonderland*, keeping up the impersonation for days at a time, and of a family joke that my elder sister would end up as matron of a girl's reformatory.

This talk of home was a help, eased my loneliness. I knew it was not polite to stay long after tea but the Champiers were unconventional, so having murmured vague words about going I lingered. Mrs Champier said, 'Do stay here if you feel like it. We go to church in the evening and my mother comes to put the children to bed. You won't be in anyone's way. We take Granny home after supper. Stay and have supper with us.' 'Yes, do stay,' said Mr Champier, 'I'd stay with you but I'm secretary of our church and have a few little duties there.' On a sudden impulse I asked, 'May I come to church with you?' It was a Methodist church, the service very like ours at home. I came away warm in spirit, loneliness forgotten.

Next morning the Adjutant sought me. 'I forgot to mention that compassionate leave allows travel warrants both ways, home and back.' Surprisingly the cost of the two long journeys had not occurred to me. Adjutants are reckoned to be a little inhuman – with all their fingers in other people's pies they acquire unique authority, apt to become autocratic. It was decent of ours to offer me travel warrants. My mind was now clear. 'Thank you, sir, but I've decided not to apply for compassionate leave.' I was certain. What comfort could it bring my parents? The inside of a week ending with another parting, my father struggling with what he would consider Christian obedience, *Thy will be done*; my mother in tears.

Of course I wrote home, cogitating a long time for healing words, but finding only conventional ones, 'greater love hath no man than to lay down his life for his friends . . . supreme sacrifice for King and country . . . his name liveth for evermore' . . . and a line recalled from doing a Shakespeare play at school (characteristically misquoted by me), 'the peace of Heaven is his who lifts his sword in such a just and charitable war.' As I licked the envelope on this dutiful letter I was slightly ashamed that my thoughts were so soon reverting to my own all-consuming passion; to my hope that I'd soon be sent out to the 64th Regiment of Foot on the Western Front.

CHAPTER TWO

The Sark Lark
and an Alderney Murder

'Three more for France,' the Adjutant told me; then stopped abruptly, seeing my hope soaring sky-high. 'No, not you yet,' he went on. 'One of them is Chapman on the Sark Detachment, and I'm sending you to take his place – at once, to-day, by fishing boat from Castle Cornet jetty, at fourteen hours . . . take all your kit. You'll be on this Sark jaunt about a month.'

In the Mess we knew that six officers were in Sark on special duty. No one knew what they did. (Jaunt! An odd word, which tripped up my thoughts.) Subalterns are always a bit cautious talking to an Adjutant but since my brother's death and the matter of compassionate leave I felt ours was less impersonal, more approachable. His next words showed he sympathized with my impatience to get to the Front, 'The war isn't going to end while you're in Sark, your turn for the *parlez-vous* will come soon enough.' (Parlez-vous! Fancy an Adjutant using our slang.)

'What happens in Sark, sir?'

'Nothing. Potty little island, hardly any people, no roads, no traffic, nowhere to go, nothing to do.' He laughed as though this unprepossessing outlook needed an extra strong full stop. (The laugh surprised me: an Adjutant's occupation doesn't encourage mirth.)

'Is it true the work is secret, sir?'

He laughed again before answering, 'Oh, very secret and

confidential. Not our responsibility, thank God! Nothing to do with the regiment really, or with the army, come to that. The French reckon Sark is within their coastal defence. Whitehall agreed to send a detachment of six trained men to patrol Sark under the orders of a French admiral. We are always short of men, and so send officers. It's an experience anyway. You are seconded for service there, so to speak.'

I must have gasped, 'The *French*? Me under command of an admiral?'

'That's the size of it. "Not though the soldier knew someone had blundered," ' he answered.

'Why an admiral?' I demanded. I was so far out of comprehension I forgot the customary 'sir'.

Casually he remarked, 'Something to do with submarines.'

Me and submarines! I'd never seen a submarine, only a picture in *The Illustrated London News*.

'Yes,' the Adjutant said with a distinct laugh, 'You'll be on patrol looking for submarines – you know, those ships which go under water so that they can't be seen.' (An Adjutant joke!) I was bold enough to join in his laugh, the whole affair too funny for words. Then he suddenly became serious, 'No more questions. I didn't intend to say so much.' His next remark, brisk, straight to the point, took away what little breath I had left. 'The QM Stores will issue you a service pistol and twenty-four rounds of ammunition. Collect them before you sail.'

He dismissed me with a comforting thought, 'Your turn for France will come. Meanwhile you'll enjoy Sark – light duties, such as they are; good rations, a proper picnic; quite a lark.' (*Lark*! What a word for an Adjutant to use.) 'Don't forget, secret and confidential – and that goes for our conversation too.'

Thus I began my Sark lark – with a Webley & Scott service pistol and twenty-four rounds. Seemed like a step towards war, rather a staggering step.

Sark is a tableland, the surface well above sea level, with cliffs like ramparts all round the island. The only harbour, named Creux ('hollow' in French), can only be used by small fishing boats at high water. It is encompassed by high cliffs, through which a narrow track leads upwards by way of a tunnel to the island's inhabited plateau. Such was the island where our detachment looked for German submarines.

Second Lieutenant Dudley, our Commander in Sark, came of a military family, was at Sandhurst when the war began, so we respected his superior military knowledge, about which however he was modestly diffident. He explained to me that he'd been to Cherbourg to meet the French admiral from whom he got orders, and to whom he had to report every week. 'A stiff old boy, Monsieur l'Amiral. My French is rotten, but we manage with an interpreter. He suspects U-boats are getting oil from Sark fishermen. Barmy idea, but "theirs not to reason why". So we do exactly what the French want. It sure is cushy. No work in the day. At night we patrol in pairs, your partner will be Kelly – you know him of course, nice bloke from Ulster.

'One night you walk at midnight to the causeway, a narrow track high above the sea which joins the two parts of the island. You stay there ten minutes looking around in case a U-boat happens to be up the cliff trying to cross the causeway. Don't say it, Old Man. We all know it's crazy. Next night is not so cushy. The two of you go to *Creux Derrible*, a huge hole sixty feet diameter, with sea one hundred and fifty feet below, washing into the hole. No fence round the rocky rim, ground uneven. There's a hut, but every half hour one or other of the patrol must go to the far end of a cliff known as Hog's Back. In places you scramble round rocks on all fours – on a dark or windy night a false step and you'd be over a precipice into the sea. That's the second night patrol, the third night you have in a comfortable bed, then the cycle starts again.'

'And we're looking for submarines? Sounds crackers to me.'

'You mustn't say that now you're in the French navy, Old Man! All this nonsense about U-boats comes from the sinking of the *Lusitania*. Politicians ignore the fact that she was bringing us food and armaments, and that we do everything we can to starve the Germans. At Sandhurst we were taught an enemy must be defeated as quickly as possible and by any means.'

'You mean all fair in love and war?'

'Can't say about love. Sandhurst didn't teach us love, concentrated on war.'

We talked of this Sark lark as barmy but I harboured a secret far-fetched hope that in some way the experience wasn't a total loss for me. For a town-bred boy accustomed to well-lit streets there was something real in scrambling along the Hog's Back on a pitch dark night, pistol in hand, ears alert for any sound above the continuous breaking of waves against the cliffs below.

Once something did happen. At breakfast the Guernsey Coastguards telephoned, 'What do you soldiers make of the vessel anchored all night off *Creux Derrible*?' Dudley looked at the two chaps who had just returned from all-night duty there. They shook their heads, swore there was no ship in sight when they came away. With commendable evasion our CO told the Coastguards he'd send them a copy of the report that he would be giving to the French in due course, if they were interested. All six of us then hurried to the Hog's Back with pistols, binoculars, a compass, and every kind of signalling equipment used by the British army.

'Looks like we'll see our first submarine,' said Kelly with Irish optimism. A few minutes later he shouted, 'There she is . . . I see her . . . quite close in shore.'

A small vessel floated in a calm sea, no smoke from the funnel, no sign of life on board. I observed, 'Small enough, but too high out of the water for a submarine, isn't she?'

Dudley said, 'Can't get down to the shore here, can't get any nearer, must rely on signalling.'

Kelly, already setting up a signal lamp, asked eagerly, 'What do we say to this submarine?'

Dudley answered, 'Soon as communication is established ask name of ship, port of registration, skipper's name, destination, nature of cargo.'

'Lummy!' exclaimed Cohen, the intellectual member of our detachment who read *Land and Water* every week, 'You've got it pat, Old Man. Where'd you pick up that nautical lore . . . holiday in Margate?'

'I know several German words, but not how to spell them,' announced Kelly very seriously.

'Use morse, that's international and English. Anyway, try it first.'

'Needn't report to Monsieur l'Amiral what *language* we use. He'll expect French, but probably be satisfied with a description of the vessel.'

Cohen said, 'Better not mention the funnel. French admirals may not like funnels on their submarines.'

We signalled with everything we'd got, using all the ways we'd been taught. I pointed out that we'd seen no one on deck, but Dudley was reluctant to give up signalling. 'Just a chance someone spots us from a hatchway. Sooner or later someone *must* come on deck; we can only watch and wait.' At last, the morning half gone, he said gloomily, 'We must shout. Only thing to do is to shout all together, damned undignified, but in war dignity must be sacrificed.' A united shout to be effective needs management – the shouters arranged in a bunch, one behind another, or all in a line. And who gives the first shout? The six of us shuffled into a row, glancing to Dudley for a lead.

'Now, all together,' he cried: but he hadn't told us *what* to shout – *ahoy!* or *hi!* or *ho!* The result was ragged. 'Again, much louder, and keep it up.' Dignity was soon lost. Someone a bit short of breath gasped, 'Damned wind . . . carries our shout inland.' The performance was not only undignified, we were conscious of looking absurd – six men in the uniform of officers standing in a group yelling for no apparent reason. Just as well there was no one to see us!

At last a protest, 'Are we going on for ever? Thirsty work. What about an adjournment for tiffin?' Reluctantly Dudley agreed, 'We'll hurry over tiffin, cut coffee and get back here as soon as possible.'

When we got back the mystery ship had vanished. 'Submerged,' pronounced Dudley, 'We've lost her. Soon as they saw the coast clear they submerged. She's now cruising away safely under water. Well, at least I've something to report to Monsieur l'Amiral.'

During the evening the Coastguards telephoned again. 'Thought you soldiers would like to know a ship turned up at St Peter's Port this afternoon . . . engine trouble yesterday, couldn't make port so anchored off *Creux Derrible* last night and spent this morning repairing the engine.' Slyly the Coastguard added, 'If you want the name for your report she's the *Sea Hawk*, registered at Jersey.' Dudley asked for some detail, then repeated to us in a low dejected voice. 'The *Sea Hawk*, registered Jersey.' Only Cohen laughed, 'A damned sea bird, and we're looking for fish.'

After my month in Sark I came back to Guernsey. In my absence three more officers had gone to France. I was now high on the list. Our training seemed to be complete. However, we were issued with military text books – *The Manual of Military Law*, *The Manual of Field Engineering* with diagrams of trenches as they should be dug, with precise measurements, and *The Manual of Military Cooking and Dietary*, including a correct form for a 'Dripping Recoveries Diary'. Some things about war had still to be mastered.

I was posted with three other subalterns to the detachment on the island of Alderney. The fort we occupied would have held a thousand men but we had only enough for guard duties at the harbour, and to keep the ramshackle place more or less clean. We took turns to be orderly officer, but had no other duties.

Garrison officers were honorary members of The Alderney Golf Club so every morning we played golf, taking the game seriously, keeping score cards, hole by hole, as though our daily play was an International Tournament. In the afternoons we swam in the sea and walked about the island which at that time had no tourists.

The Manual of Military Law is the army's Bible. Every officer had a copy. I never saw anyone reading it. I didn't open my copy till one of the men committed murder. The incident occurred one dark night when I was going to inspect the guard beyond the harbour entrance. A strong wind swept the narrow break-water so that I was obliged to crouch low to avoid being blown into the sea. The blackness ahead was suddenly broken by a bright light from the Guard Room door. We didn't fuss about blackout rules, but this was more than a bit careless. I saw a figure running in my direction. When some thirty yards away he saw me, guessed I was the orderly officer and shouted:

'Sergeant wants you, sir . . . been a murder.'

'Been a what?'

'Murder, sir . . . a murder.'

The sergeant was kneeling beside a body on the floor of the Guard Room. He shook his head at me – means the chap's dead, I thought. I could see the fellow was unconscious – eyes shut, jaw dropped, mouth wide open with a trickle of blood coming from one corner. I'd never seen a dead man. How could the sergeant be so sure he was dead? How does one know for certain? Another body lay on the floor, alive, twitching shoulders shaking from uncontrolled weeping. Three other of the guard, crammed together on a bench, stared in silence – at the sergeant, at the murdered man, at the murderer, and now at me.

The sergeant stood up. 'Thank God you've come, sir.' Little enough to thank the Almighty for, I reflected grimly. I was nonplussed, never been in such a situation. 'Job for an MO,' the sergeant hazarded, 'only doctor in the island lives next the pub, opposite the Post Office in St Anne.'

It was up to me to give some order. Tentatively I asked, 'Could one of the guard go to the Officers' Mess at the fort, tell them what's happened . . . ?' But the NCO cut me short, 'Quicker if he goes straight to the doctor.' He pointed to one of the men on the bench. 'Private Dawson's reliable, sir.' Without giving me time to assent he shouted, 'Dawson, on your feet man. You know the pub, even if you've forgotten your own name. Doctor's next door . . . knock him up, tell him the officer wants him here at the double . . . tell him it's a murder – murder always gets a medico out of his nightshirt and on the road.'

When Dawson had gone the sergeant gently kicked the sobbing man on the floor, 'This one won't be no trouble, sir, a timid lad, too shy even to go after a girl. But p'raps you ought to put 'im under arrest, sir?' He paused, expecting me to proclaim the arrest. How does one do that? I pictured a judge at the Old Bailey putting on a black cap. The sergeant went on, 'Natur-ally, lads like 'im gets put upon in the army but this one', touching the dead man, 'was his friend . . . kept an eye on 'im to jump in with help when any horse-play went over the top, as you might say, sir.'

'But what *happened*, sergeant?'

30

'Been on rifle range today, sir. Men don't get so much of that as they'd like. Damned good shots some of 'em. This poor bastard a wash-out, fired three times, never hit the bloody target. Tonight some of the guard made fun of him, mocked him – couldn't hit a haystack five yards away . . . shoot his own brains out if he weren't more careful . . . silly talk like that. Surprisingly, his friend joined the others against him. Told him he was afraid of the kick from the rifle. You know, sir, some recruits is like that when they first go on the range. Well, suddenly the poor bastard pointed his rifle at his friend crying, "I'll show you if I'm afraid of the kick." What you'd call unpremeditated, sir.'

'He fired *once?*' I asked.

'Once . . . and he didn't miss the target.'

Unpremeditated was right; instinct to hit back, and the more powerful in a mild man because long suppressed.

'Not fear which makes him blub now,' reflected the sergeant. 'He don't think of what's coming to him. Next time he hears a rifle shot it'll be a firing squad. The army don't hang murderers like civvies do, we shoot 'em before breakfast.'

My *Manual of Military Law* was doing temporary service in my room as a tie press, but during the next few days I skipped through its pages to see what it said about murder. Every fourth day, as orderly officer, I had to visit the murderer in his cell. The orderly sergeant unlocked the door, did a loud rat-tat-tat with a swagger cane, and shouted 'Shun!' The lad leapt to his feet and stood to attention as he'd been drilled, waiting for me to speak. I wanted to say a word of comfort, but couldn't find one. The sergeant turned his face to me, reminding me of my duty.

'Any complaints?'

No, of course not. What could a murderer possibly have to complain about? I walked away, the sergeant relocked the door, the solitary confinement went on. Meanwhile, the army became involved in an acrimonious dispute with the Alderney Civil Authorities who claimed murder must be tried under Civil Law and, moreover, by some fifteenth-century body known as the *Estate Generaux*. The lawyers on both sides – civil and military – were not prepared to forego their rights – both wanted to execute this man who was too shy to go after a girl. God knows how it ended. In the army we are here today, gone tomorrow. Suddenly I was ordered to go to France – to the Front, my Mecca, to the very heart of war, where men are shot in thousands, and an odd murder isn't worth any further recording.

CHAPTER THREE

The Way to Shrapnel Corner

In a state of ecstasy I went my way to the Western Front. The Greek origin of the word was not belied: I stood outside myself, lifted above normal senses – the swell of the sea, the taste of salt on my lips, the sight of an endless succession of crested waves coming from nowhere and hurrying away to another nowhere, strange nautical sounds which haunt ships as ghost-sounds haunt old houses. These physical sensations were magnified immensely by my comprehending ecstasy. Everyone and everything collaborated to enlarge my awareness.

An elderly sergeant at the Quartermaster's Stores in Southampton docks provided me with items of kit and equipment, explaining each in a pleasing manner, blending deference and familiarity.

1 Gas mask in waterproof satchel: 'Wouldn't open it up here, sir, this new type a bit awkward to refold, needs a bit of practice. You can do that when you get to trenches, more than enough time to spare there, sir.'

2 Pistol ammunition: 'I'd keep the ammunition separate, sir, till you come where you may 'ave to shoot.'

3 Field Service Notebook: 'Sort of extracts on military law and practical notes on warfare.'

4 Bandage: 'Fits pocket inside your jacket, sir, and with it this tube of iodine – wonderful stuff to swab on wounds.'

5 Identity Disc: 'I'll fetch that now, sir. They've been stamping on the details.'

I hadn't heard of identity discs. Why hadn't anyone told me? Obviously necessary to identify everyone on active service. And ecstasy made mine a badge of honour, as good as any medal. 'Put it round your neck now, sir, make sure it hangs comfortable. Where you're going, sir, baths are a luxury, but *any* time you happen to take your clothes off, keep the disc on.' With a smile he added, 'Remember sir, without this disc you are anybody; with it you are yourself and nobody else.' After my name, rank and regiment, the letters C of E were stamped clearly into the metal.

'Why do you put a chap's religion on the disc, sergeant?'

He laughed. 'Precaution, sir, precaution. In war you never can tell.'

'Tell what?'

'Why, sir, if your number *should* happen to come up, you wouldn't want the chaplains to quarrel about who's to bury you.'

'I'm not really C of E.' I observed mildly.

The sergeant said in the tone of a wise man talking to an inexperienced youth, 'You stick to C of E, sir. You wouldn't want to be buried by the Pope I'm sure.'

I laughed. 'I don't suppose it makes any difference.'

'Oh, it does make a difference, sir.' He spoke earnestly. 'It does. RCs go to Hell before they get to Heaven – that's official. RCs call it Purgatory. You're definitely better off as C of E, sir.'

This small error on my disc did nothing to dampen my elation. I thought how my father would have wanted it corrected. 'Never sail under false colours,' he'd have said, but I wasn't going to risk any possible delay in my sailing. And I saw the matter in a practical way. What difference can it make when you're dead, how you are buried, or by whom? Before I'd even landed in France I had a new habit – pushing a finger through my jacket and through the shirt, just to touch the disc

34

which distinguished me from everyone else in the world. As the QM sergeant said – without the disc I was anybody; with it I was myself, nobody else.

On the 29th April, 1916, I had my first sight of France. The troopship berthed at a wharf right in the city of Le Havre. I looked down from the ship's deck on a kind of square, the Place de la Gare, fringed with a row of tamarisk trees, with buildings, shops and offices on one side, and advertisement hoardings on the other. The scene was one of great activity, men, women and children going about their customary affairs. The few men (most are fighting, I thought) wore coloured blouses like women. The women, outnumbering the men at least five to one, dressed in ankle-length bright garments, a few in black (mourning for men killed in the war, I thought). The many children shouting loudly, rushed about armed with bits of wood, or sticks, fighting the imaginary battles of childhood. Strong smells drifted my way – smoke from the railway, bread from a bakery, fish set out on a long street stall. The general impression was one of many activities, everyone doing some-thing felt to be necessary and important.

My school French guessed some of the words on the advertis-ing hoardings:– *savon*, *tabac*, *parfum*, *vin* and *bière*. As I looked further around I saw flaming red letters over the railway station. *Taisez-vous, méfiez-vous, les oreilles de l'ennemi vous écoutent.* I had forgotten the silly spy scares at home in the early days of war. Now I was in a country where war was a reality; here anyone could be a spy – that train shunter in a blue blouse blowing a comic little horn, uniformed officials beside a troop train in a siding, with trucks inscribed *Hommes 40, Chevaux en long 8*, or the big navvy emptying buckets of water into the sea as though he had an ocean to fill, or the fellow leaning against an office wall puffing a cigar or even the girl from a *boulangerie*, her bare arms embracing yard-long rolls of bread; any one of these could be a German spy. *Les oreilles de l'ennemi vous écoutent.*

Passports were unknown in 1916 and I had no luggage to go through Customs – only a valise (my bed at night, my chest of drawers by day). As I waited for the order to go ashore I felt my pockets for my pipe and tobacco, my wallet with a few army papers and French francs – nothing else but a Boot's Pocket Diary given me at Christmas by my younger sister. Not a proper diary, only a small space for notes, a whole week on a page. I glanced at what I had already written since the year began – a few football results, Alderney Detachment v. Alderney Civilians, reminders of family birthdays (an aunt's on 9th January, my grandmother 24th February, grandfather 8th March and my father 23rd March), a picnic with two girls of Alderney Badminton Club; almost all about family or friends. At Southampton docks I'd been parted from the other chaps who came with me from the Channel Islands, I was alone in a foreign land and although in a mood of ecstasy I appreciated these old diary entries as almost news.

Diaries were not allowed at the Front. I intended to get rid of this one before I reached the trenches, which might be two or three weeks. But I reflected that one of my duties would be to censor the letters my men wrote to their wives, parents and friends, deleting anything which might help enemy intelligence. Surely, I said to myself, I must be capable of censoring what I jot down in my own personal diary! So it came about that when I went home on leave six months later in the month of October, I took my diary with me and returned with a fresh one. A similar swap on a second leave in 1917 means that I now have a continuous record, written day-by-day, throughout the fifteen months of my active service. The short entries are of no historical value, being mainly personal and about unmilitary events like football matches, church parades, and conditions which at the time struck me as a bit unusual, such as: '9th

September, first bath since 15th July'. Some pages record the names of brother-officers killed or wounded on that day: '1st September 2 killed, 1 missing, 5 wounded', occasionally names of men killed to remind me of letters of condolence I must write to next-of-kin. 3rd September has the names of ten in my platoon killed during the night.

In 1916 no one took much interest in Intelligence or Security but later out battalion had its own Intelligence Officer at Battalion HQ.

In the Channel Islands I'd seen only men of my own regiment. At No. 6 Infantry Base on the outskirts of Rouen, to which I went from Le Havre, men came from many regiments: English, Scots, Welsh, Irish, colonials from Australia, New Zealand, Canada and South Africa (to my astonishment I heard Canadians being drilled with French words of command – men from Quebec, I was told) even contingents of brown men of the Indian Army, black men in the uniform of the West African Rifles, and some yellow from parts of Asia. Exhilarating to be one of such a great army, fighting to liberate little Belgium from the infamous German Huns.

Even as I glowed with excitement I was conscious of fringe questions, not yet in definite words but unlikely to fade away without some answers. Why so many, far from the trenches? How long before we moved on? Rouen was miles from where we knew the British army was fighting. I found myself sitting next to an Artillery chap in the Officers' canteen and boldly asked what he was doing at an Infantry Depot. 'Same as most of the infantry – which is Damn All.' He was amused at my concern to get to the Front. 'You needn't fear the war will end soon,' he assured me, 'not with the shortage of shells. Bosche are short too. With us it's chronic, my battery is rationed, only allowed to fire a few shells per day; like fighting with one arm tied behind you.' He went on to speak of thousands of men doing duties outside the war area – transport, catering, stores, various HQ officials, and staff officers, not to mention a few hundred thousand cavalry made obsolete by trenches. This aspect of the war was new to me.

Later I overheard bits of conversation which damped down my ecstasy:

'If I could be sure I'd be here in Rouen for the duration I'd marry the girl, take her back to Blighty when we go.'

'All a matter of luck, Old Man, I've been here three months, some chaps are sent up the line after only three days.'

'Typical army – here today, gone tomorrow. And others forgotten, presumed dead, so to say.'

'Can't do anything about it. Seems like a kid's game, you have to throw a six before you can move.'

'How right you are – only it's some damned Brass Hat who throws for you.'

I was in France but not at the Front, not even within the sound of distant gunfire. It would be tragic to be stuck at a base depot while the war petered out. The weekly, *Land and Water* (reporting Germans starved and lacking essential products like lubricating oils) wrote hopefully of the war ending as suddenly as it began. To me this seemed an ironic possibility – a post-war life in the company of scrimshankers who had dodged war at a base depot and, of course, fellows of another generation too young to have experienced anything.

Whoever threw the dice for me threw a six next day. In a few hours I was on the way to Poperinghe, the rail-head for Ypres (known as 'Wipers' or simply 'The Salient'), reputedly the most blood-soaked soil in Europe. I was never again in a base depot.

My train to Poperinghe stopped short of the station, setting before my startled eyes a panorama of chaos – a derailed train with carriages overturned across a great hole in the permanent way; a large signal box now a heap of charred timber with contorted machinery sticking from it; station buildings with holes in roofs and walls, and broken glass everywhere. This, my first sight of war damage, was a shock. In my daydreaming of war, men fought one another with rifles and bayonets and pistols, but somehow I hadn't thought of material destruction, or rather my imagination hadn't got that far. In England I'd once seen slum houses being pulled down with pick and shovel, but otherwise only ancient ruins of historic interest, no modern buildings or up-to-date machinery deliberately destroyed – wanton barbarity!

The Railway Transport Officer was to direct me to our first battalion, somewhere in the Front Line.

'Sorry I can't offer you any transport,' he said sardonically, 'must apologise for the untidiness of my station, all done by our Little Willie . . . but you've only just come from Blighty, won't have heard of Little Willie, the biggest gun ever made, taken off one of Tirpitz's battleships now blockaded in the Kiel Canal. Germans set up Little Willie on land, miles t'other side of No-Man's-Land. Fortunately he's very inaccurate, usually well off target, shells fall mostly in open country, harmless. But when Little Willie's luck is in he can do a hell of a lot of damage, as you may have noticed. No joke if you happen to be around.' He turned over some papers. '64th Foot for you,' he said. 'They are beyond Wipers, near Shrapnel Corner. A pleasant walk, take best part of a day. Better spend the night here, they'll put you up at Toc H and you can make an early start tomorrow.'

Toc H was a kind of hostel for the British Army opened in Poperinghe as a memorial to a popular chaplain killed early in the war. During the evening I went up to an attic there called

39

'The Upper Room', a chapel with an altar (a packing case still labelled 'jam – plum and apple'). A notice on the door gave times of Holy Communion, and an invitation to all Christians regardless of denomination, 'to join with us at the Lord's Table'. A welcome surprise for a non-conformist, but what thrilled me more was a prominent slogan over the door of the chaplain's room, *All rank abandon ye who enter here* – Dante's famous words turned upside down and inside out, a brilliant thought, a challenge to army conventions and traditions. To me, an Englishman schooled in Scotland, it was an affirmation of the great words of Burns, 'A prince can make a belted knight a marquis, duke, and a' that . . . the rank is but the guinea's stamp . . . a man's a man for a' that.' I was staring at the slogan, the very centre of my mind aglow, when a voice behind me said, 'For or against? I like to know how it strikes a newcomer.' I think he was the warden. I seized one of his hands and cried, 'A stroke of genius . . . your idea I suppose?'

'Hardly genius. When we were adapting this place for Toc H I met an officer fresh from the trenches. He talked about the strange conditions of trench life, so totally different from ordinary life, so unlike what civilians suppose. I was struck by one of his observations: he said that in a trench crisis, a life-and-death emergency, every man is judged by his character, not by his rank. That's what gave me the idea.'

'Does it work?' He took my arm and led me to the room which had been the salon in peacetime. He opened the door, looked round and nodded, drawing attention to two men, sitting side by side in close conversation – one a captain, the other a private. In the canteen I saw an officer, a corporal and four privates all together at the counter. Unthinkable in Blighty; where since the war social distinctions were rigidly maintained by 'Officers Only' notices at the entrance to many hotels, restaurants, bars and even tea shops. What the war ought to be doing, I thought, is reducing class barriers, making less difference between rich and poor – the rank is but the guinea's stamp.

A fine sunny morning when I left the railhead to walk towards Ypres, on the way to Shrapnel Corner: a long road across a wide plain, no buildings, no trees except an avenue of precisely spaced Lombardy Poplars which tucked in the road, so to say; no abrupt turnings, no side tracks, no ups, no downs. A road not to be taken casually, the first step obviously committing one to going on to some end. The unbounded plain, with no dividing hedges or fences, grew mixed crops, wheat, oats, barley, potatoes and general vegetables: the bounty of Nature rewarding thousands of years of man's toil.

A kilometre or so outside Poperinghe I was overtaken by a large man in a small cart, pulled by two dogs. He waved as he passed, shouted a few words I didn't understand. A farmer, I supposed, evacuated to the safe side of Poperinghe, and coming into the danger zone for the day. After he disappeared I had the road to myself, no traffic, no pedestrians, and a great silence in the empty land, save only for the singing of larks, carrying their jubilant song heavenwards. Perhaps larks have always liked this large flat treeless country and stuck to it in spite of being so near to war.

The Transport chap said it would take me the best part of a day to reach Shrapnel Corner. Well, route-marches in Guernsey had accustomed me to long treks. I was elated, outside myself, very carefree so I whistled march tunes as I walked – *Tipperary*, *Keep the Home Fires Burning* and the popular *There's a long long trail a-winding*. Another part of my mind reflected how little I'd imagined I would walk alone this last bit of the way to war. I don't quite know what I'd expected, marching at the head of a platoon I suppose. Perhaps I hadn't imagined any details.

I was surprised to come upon a man at work, hoeing a patch of cabbages. He moved one step at a time, head bowed, eyes on the ground: one old man with a hoe in a vast field, seven maids with seven mops! And I had thought myself the only living creature hereabouts. He took no notice of me.

Suddenly the peace was shattered, horror fell upon me – my first shell: a monster tearing through the air like an express railway train out of control, menacing, demanding attention. I don't know how I realised it was a shell. I'd supposed that a shell would just arrive and burst, the burst being what mattered. No one had warned me the thing tells you it's coming – a small distant sound swelling steadily, louder and faster, still louder and still faster, approaching at incredible speed, all the while prolonging the tension. Seconds and fractions of a second are measures of conventional time; as soon as one hears an approaching shell the mind turns to true time, time as it seems to the hearer. I guessed this shell was one of Little Willie's, intended for Poperinghe, falling short . . . falling . . . on me. Terror mounted, but a significant sound, a hard dry cough, registered itself on the edge of my mind, the sound of the gun firing kilometres away, sound travelling at ground level arriving while the shell is still rumbling along its high trajectory up in the sky. That edge-thought was not sufficient to lessen the fear which took possession of the centre of my mind. I flung myself on the ground, pressing my body to the earth passionately. The world shuddered beneath me, a roar assailed my ears, my head seemed split. Fragments of metal, stone, lumps of earth, stabbed the air in all directions. I felt a blow in the small of my back, and a sharp stinging crack on a shoulder. Then total silence – peace holding her breath to make sure violence was exhausted.

A single lark broke the silence, aware that someone must be first to recover normality; other larks were quick to follow, not in chorus for larks are individualists, but soon the air was saturated with jubilant song. Fear still claimed me, but a different fear, the rational fear of being seen to be afraid, a coward. This powerful fear picked me up, stood me on my feet, turned my face towards the only man in sight. Was he a coward too? Had he thrown himself to the ground amongst his cabbages, dropped his hoe? He was walking towards me. I could see his face now, a leathery face with the look of a countryman accustomed to the sharp practices of the market place. He was jabbering at me, at first I thought in hostility. I caught the words *na pooh* and *Bosche*. I looked in the direction he pointed – the yard-high rim of the shell hole. He was shaking his fist towards it, and every time he said 'Bosche' he stopped to spit. His tirade ended abruptly, as though he realised he'd used up a reasonable ration of hate. His face uncreased into a smile, a large smile which set the smaller wrinkles round his eyes and lips moving like ripples on a windswept pond. 'Na pooh, Bosche,' he cried, and then, 'Que voulez-vous, M'sieur?' He laughed, 'Que voulez-vous? C'est la guerre.'

Fie my lord, fie! a soldier and afeared?, but Macbeth's hands were bloody, mine only gritty from scratching the earth. My thoughts were shaken, jumbled together in no order, facts with no conclusions, feelings beyond common-sense; all dominated by fear.

'A thousand shall fall at thy side, but it shall not come nigh thee . . .' Won't it? Not another Little Willie shell from that innocent blue sky, a shell eighteen inches in diameter and God knows how long? The old Psalmist hadn't heard of Little Willie!

I am a coward . . . rushed to arms with patriotic fervour, proud to fight in a noble cause, to defeat the German aggressor. What had gone wrong? Germans are men like us, with the strength and weakness and limitations of mankind. I could do battle with men but this pistol at my side is no weapon to aim at some ineluctable power from the sky. How many rounds from a Webley & Scott would stop an earthquake, or a volcano? In trenches most shells won't be so large as Little Willie but I shall listen in fear to every single one coming my way, knowing I have nothing with which to fight super-human forces. At school in 1914 I was crazy to be a hero, but it turns out I am a coward. Some chaps never grow up, always want to be heroes. Not me, not any longer. I just can't face War.

Click . . . click . . . click, the peasant back at his everlasting task, his hoe clicking stones in the cabbage bed. He and I, within handshake, but really centuries apart. 'Que voulez-vous? C'est la guerre' – that's all war means to him, an interruption in producing the first essential for human life, as it was in the beginning, is now, and ever shall be. And I, a soldier, am very much afeared – a coward, a dithering coward, not knowing what to do next, or where to go. I supposed this man to be an ignorant peasant content to let others fight for his freedom: but he *is* free, comes here day by day, disregarding war as his ancestors have done for a thousand years; war no concern of theirs, brought to them from afar by foreigners, 'Que voulez-vous?' Only a never-ending, 'click . . . click . . . click' and the larks singing their way heavenwards, jubilant of Life.

At length my fear was overlaid by shame. I resumed my walk to Shrapnel Corner, rather unsteadily. Where else could I go?

'As you approach Wipers you'll see the ruins of a large asylum – the loony-bin. Most Belgians are loony, could have done with a bin twice that size.' So said the RTO chap in Poperinghe. 'Opposite those ruins an army sign points to Shrapnel Corner, you'll be in the trenches tomorrow. Can't miss Shrapnel Corner.' Like any sensible man using that 'can't miss' phrase, he had sketched for me a map, on the back of a railway circular advertising excursions from Zeebrugge to London. How far had I come along that road? He'd written the name of a village a few kilometres before Wipers . . . not easy to read his writing, but the indistinct letters all at once sorted themselves into a name I recognised – Vlamertinghe: a corner of a foreign land forever England, the place where my brother is buried.

At home my father and I had searched an atlas in vain for Vlamertinghe, an important spot for us, to the world at large an insignificant village. And I had stumbled on the place as I walked: not much of a coincidence because Vlamertinghe was the only place between Poperinghe and Wipers. On the outskirts of this deserted village I saw a small fenced-off part of the wide Flanders Plain, obviously a war cemetery: thirty or forty temporary wooden crosses, evenly spaced, all upright, standing to attention as though waiting for someone to come and inspect them – an archangel perhaps. From where I stood I couldn't read the names painted below the crosses, but one would be the name of my brother. A wholly unexpected encounter, this meeting with my brother, dead six months and not spoken with since before the war.

I stepped over a little ditch beside the road to go closer, and then stopped involuntarily. I don't know what held me. I stood, maybe a full minute, on the short path leading to the graves. My mind wasn't blank, I wasn't dazed or shocked, but I found it difficult to concentrate; thoughts were disconnected, and faded away unfinished. My own living body seemed unreal, without substance, as moving in a dream one is unhampered even when bumping into physical objects. I found myself on the road again, evidently I'd turned back without walking those last few steps.

Perhaps I turned from my brother's grave because graves are silent, and I wanted to talk as we used to talk together in our school days, telling each other of hopes, and doubts, and fears. So much I had to tell, so many questions to ask. 'Died of wounds', what sort of wounds? Died in the front line? Or in some field ambulance, or hospital? And why Vlamertinghe, so far from any trenches? I knew I must explain to him that I am a coward, all I'd written in letters about longing to get to the Front was only a passion, a feeling, sentiment. Of course I really meant every word, but now I was here I'd discovered I was a coward. I wouldn't have even got to Vlamertinghe if I had not been shamed by an intrepid and ignorant peasant, with his 'Que voulez-vous? C'est la guerre'.

I walked on through the empty village, troubled a little by a silence which seemed to blanket the whole countryside of Flanders, as though Nature were taking a nap, disgusted with the goings-on of *homo sapiens*. What had become of those skylarks, singing their way up and up and up to heaven? Had they reached the pearly gates? Was this the silence of re-nounced Life? I stood listening intently. From somewhere ahead my ears picked up a sound they'd never heard before, a new sound to me, as a child hears thunder for the first time before anyone has named it. But I knew the name of this thunder: the rumble of continuous gunfire, calling me to a duty I had reason to dread.

CHAPTER FOUR

A Ditch Across Europe

A trench newspaper, *The Wipers Times*, printed in 'a rat-infested waterlogged cellar' of Ypres, describes trench war at the date when I got there.

> Take a wilderness of ruin, spread with
>   mud quite six feet deep;
> In this mud now cut some channels, then
>   you have the line we keep.
> Get a lot of Huns and plant them, in a
>   ditch across the way;
> Now you have war in the making, as waged
>   from day to day.

Unlike anything I'd imagined, unlike the war for which I had been trained. I was very much the new boy, arriving at a new school. No moving cinema pictures, no ordinary photographs or any visual aids to help imagination. I had never seen a trench map, or a photo from the air, or any official notes describing the Front; no war-correspondents, only a few journalists writing up official communiqués in the London daily newspapers, men who had never themselves been near a trench.

The *Manual of Field Engineering*, issued to infantry subalterns, was no help. The front trench, where we lived, had been dug in the early days of the war by troops under fire. Irregular in depth and width, it had suffered many direct hits by enemy shells and was more or less always under repair. Somehow I had assumed continuous gunfire at the Front, shells falling on the trenches all day, and of course a regular rattle of rifle and machine gun fire.

It was almost disquieting (so to say) to be told there were long periods when war was silent. But the front trench usually had a daily concentrated *strafe* lasting perhaps fifteen to thirty minutes and some intermittent shelling at Dawn-Stand-To and Dusk-Stand-To when all troops were on duty, an hour each period. A communication trench connected the front trench with Battalion HQ, a small group of dug-outs four or five hundred yards back, where the Colonel, Second-in-Command and Adjutant lived with attendant staff. All supplies, rations and relieving troops used this communication trench under cover of darkness but in some places it was reasonably safe for one or two to use it by day.

The Adjutant gave me an outline of the general routine of the battalion and concluded, 'We are short of officers. You are posted to D Company, commanded by 2nd Lieutenant Hardy. He'll show you the ropes, some of which will surprise you. Hardy is out-spoken but very experienced, been out three months.' The phrase 'been out', indicating the time since a man joined the army in France, was in common use amongst infantry in trenches. I had been out 'less than a week' – no experience at all. The Adjutant rightly called Hardy 'very experienced'. He was three years older than me and ten months senior in army rank, a tall man, with a long face, a high brow and alert eyes. In his presence it was difficult to attend to anyone else.

At first I was intimidated by Hardy, a little frightened, but definitely impressed. He was direct in speech, dogmatic and until I knew him well he seemed to speak only in what I thought of as 'outbursts'.

'You straight from Blighty, so you won't know a damned thing. None of us did when we came out. Not your fault. You will take over 13 platoon which has been run by Sergeant Hill since the last officer got a Blighty wound – and Hill has run the platoon damned well. You can rely on him to put you wise.' He added in the manner of a judge giving advice to a convict before passing sentence, 'But 13 platoon is *your* responsibility. Hill will tell you what you need to know but you are in command.'

And so it happened. Hill told me my duties, explained carefully this strange new world and even considered my personal safety. 'Seems a natural impulse to take a quick look over the trench parapet in daylight,' he warned, 'but an impulse to resist. In most parts of the line it would be risky, hereabouts fatal. Very active snipers over the way. Our chaps call snipers *notchers*, believe they cut a notch on the rifle butt for every man they kill. They insist there is only one *notcher* on the look-out here; call him *Top-notcher*. If I may suggest it, sir, don't ever look over the top in daylight, not for a second. *Top-notcher* might get you!'

Hill had been using a little dug-out intended for the platoon commander. He handed it over with the comment, 'Bit small, sir, but room for you to lie slantwise; good roof; walls reinforced with cement scrounged from REs; floor above level of duck-board . . . shouldn't be flooded this time o' year; in fact as good a dug-out as I've seen around here. Can't say it has *all modern conveniences* – Mr Hardy showed you Officers' Latrine I expect, behind Company Headquarters. There *are* disadvantages – chicken wire across the roof is low because the rats have a highway running just over where your head comes when you lie down – the wire keeps them from actually running over you.' I had seen several huge rats scurrying about, and decided I didn't like the creatures; very romantic in children's stories, but . . . Sergeant Hill added in a voice charged with feeling – 'Rats are bloody hell. A corporal in A Company was bitten when asleep – the MO had to put a stitch in his nose.'

I was a little unhappy to be taking over the platoon comman-der's super dug-out and asked Hill where he would sleep. He

replied lightly, 'Oh, I can look after myself, sir. None of us get
more than two or three hours off duty at a stretch and that not
at night. You need a dug-out to yourself, for personal belong-
ings, your pack, and some official records and army forms: the
rest of us share dug-outs when we get the chance of a short nap.
Battalion does six days and nights here, then a spell in Support
trenches five hundred yards back, that's where we get a real
kip.' He pointed to several dug-outs used by men and NCOs –
very small, room for three or four men to lie side by side, dug
out from the back of the trench or in a short sap, with sandbag
protection above, sometimes reinforced by a baulk of timber or
scrap metal.

As I moved around the trench on my first day Sergeant Hill
was my shadow, always close, always quick to murmur advice,
not officious. I never met a more intelligent NCO. I understood
why Hardy warned me to show no hesitation in taking command, my coming inevitably reduced Hill's accustomed authority. He was a natural leader, would have made an excellent
officer if he had been born in the right social class. (Later I had
a letter from his father, well expressed, correctly written, but on
notepaper headed in print with his name and occupation –
Undertaker.)

That first evening I had a meal with Hardy in Company HQ
dug-out. I mentioned what Hill said about *notchers* and asked,
'What happens when we go over the top?' My question
triggered an outburst.

'In practice the fighting takes place in two parallel ditches
(ours and the enemy's) running across Europe, hundreds of
kilometres long, in a strip less than five kilometres wide.
Outside these ditches there is no war, beyond them civilians go
on living in peace. We *Poor Bloody Infantry* are the men who
matter. Our job is to hold the line, prevent an enemy breakthrough. Talk of going over the top is only Glory-War talk,

patriotic twaddle. The German people are starving; time is on our side. Got that? We PBI don't kill (very seldom anyway; we're the chaps who are killed. Killing is done by artillery (almost all anyway). Guns pound us, from two or three kilometres behind the trenches; usually the gunners can't see us, often don't know where their shells fall. Your platoon holds about one hundred yards of the long ditch, a short length but vital. Let the enemy through there and all the King's horses (the cavalry) and all the King's men (RA, RFC, RE, and the rest) couldn't put Humpty Dumpty together again. Your job, holding a vital link in the long chain which blockades the enemy, is too important for Glory-War, going over the top and all that.'

This outburst impressed me. Hardy must be exaggerating, using hyperbole to stress what he considered important for me to grasp, but what I'd learned from Sergeant Hill gave it some credence and the notion that I had full responsibility for even a short distance of the trench system remained with me for the whole of my service on the Western Front. I still remember some of Hardy's other pithy observations:

Army commanders write long books on Strategy and tactics, but all their military science is bunk. Real war is confusion and muddle from the first shot fired to the armistice at the end.

War isn't like the text-books issued from the War Office. For centuries men have fought on horseback, now cavalry are obsolete, useless against foot soldiers in trenches. We don't even march four-deep down communication trenches, or form close column of platoons and charge across No-Man's-Land. In trenches we don't salute or stand to attention.

In trenches we are like convicts in Wormwood Scrubs, closely confined – by the enemy across No-Man's-Land, by other units on both flanks. Any attempt to retreat ends in Court Martial and death penalty. We are fed and watered by the commissariat, have no shops, no music halls, no cinemas, use no money. No one visits us in the front line – not generals, or staff officers, or chaplains, or even doctors. We don't know what is happening in the world beyond our prison. Ours is the privacy of a cemetery. When we die we sometimes have to bury ourselves.

German army is best trained in the world but creatures of habit, apt to put on a strafe same time every day and shell a target, like the Menin Gate or Shrapnel Corner, at regular intervals – one shell every so many seconds or minutes, thus forfeiting the element of surprise. But their generals are properly trained and damned good soldiers. Fact is we picked the wrong allies, ought to be fighting with the Germans against the French.

I was nineteen years old, afraid of having my leg pulled in this strange new world. Looking back I know I was lucky to encounter Hardy and Hill during my first three days. At the time I thought Hardy couldn't really mean all that he said . . . or did he? I remembered the Adjutant's remark, 'outspoken but very experienced'.

My second night was a fine clear one with a full moon. Hill encouraged me to climb out of the trench for a quick look at our wire protection. He explained that regular inspection was desirable so that 'gooseberries' (round barbed-wire balls about three feet in diameter) could be constructed in the trench by day and fixed at night to the main picket-irons if the wire had been damaged by shell fire. I had a feeling that Hill took me out to our barbed wire chiefly to encourage me, show me that at night some activities above ground were possible. 'If Jerry puts up a Very-Light, sir, stand stock still till it has burned out, the slightest movement would be spotted by a *notcher*, but if you don't move there's little risk.' Later, when the moon had set, Hill handed me a Very pistol. 'We've four of these pistols in the platoon,' he said, 'keep this for your own use, sir, take it with you always at night.' As I examined the pistol (I'd never seen one before) he added, 'Try a shot now, sir.' I pointed skyward across towards the Bosche front line and pressed the trigger. While the soft light floated above No-Man's-Land and we stared, looking to spot an enemy patrol or other movement, I told myself it was my first act in war: not exactly fighting, but a definite act. Hill observed, 'Very pistols not reckoned as weapons, sir, but need to be handled with care, at short range could kill a man.'

On the morning of my third day Battalion HQ issued the warning *Gas Alert*. 'Only a precaution, sir,' explained Sergeant Hill. 'Wind changed direction during the night, a light breeze now blowing towards us across No-Man's-Land. When so we always wear masks in the ready position.' He saw that I didn't know anything about the ready position. My mask was a hood of flannel or some such material to cover the whole head, with a mouth piece and two eye pieces. 'It's a new type, sir. On *Gas Alert* we pin the front edge to the shirt with two safety pins, fold the mask over the chest, and button the top button of the tunic. On the warning, *Gas Alarm*, you only need to unbutton the tunic and the mask falls open ready to pull over the head.' He demonstrated with my mask and concluded, 'There you are, sir. All we have to do now is to make sure the men are at *Gas Alert*. I carry a few extra safety pins with me, they are as you might say the linch-pins of the whole operation; always some careless fellow who has lost his pins. Wonder is how some men keep alive in this wicked world.'

At intervals along the trench gas gongs were hung, with metal rods or tools beside them. These gongs were shell cases from gun batteries to be banged if at any time a cloud of gas was seen approaching. Hill pointing at a gong said, 'Actually gas attacks are rare, sir, I've never been in one. Damned unpleasant I guess and can cause a lot of casualties. Mr Hardy says there won't be any more, don't know why he's so sure about it.' He grinned, as sharing a confidence. 'A clever gentleman, Mr Hardy, but he does have some rum ideas, as I expect you've discovered, sir?'

My third day in trenches was followed by a fine cloudless night, the sky's wealth of stars diminished only by the brightness of a full moon. After the day's warmth the air struck cold. I walked up the short communication trench to Company HQ to ask the batman to brew me a hot drink. While waiting I stood outside the dug-out where a slope in the ground gave me a long view, a jumble of shapeless earthworks down behind the front trench. I could hear some of the common sounds of trench life – an occasional rifle shot, machine gun fire casually sweeping No-Man's-Land in the hope of catching a wiring party at work, thuds as full sandbags were dumped to repair gaps caused by a shell, the scrape of a spade turning over excrement in a latrine.

Our forefathers attributed all manner of strange powers to the moon. A Psalmist declared, *The Lord is thy defence; so that the sun shall not burn thee by day, neither the moon by night*. Even in our scientific age moon-superstitions persist, but no one now thinks the moon can burn anyone. The moon has never been a threat to mankind. I stared at its full round orb, moonstruck as a child trying to see the man in the moon.

The batman brought me a steaming hot mug of cocoa. 'Thanks,' I said and added casually by way of friendly talk, 'this moonshine covers the ugliness of trenches. How quiet it is.'

'Not all that quiet, sir. Sounds as if someone was copping something way over beyond Sanctuary Wood.'

We stood listening a moment. Certainly the gunfire was persistent and coming more our way. The batman returned to the dug-out, jerking the gas blanket a little to one side as a hint to me. 'Best come in out of the cold, sir.' But I was still moonstruck, recalling words of a modern poet: 'The innocent moon which nothing does but shine.' How *very* innocent the moon is! Unlike the energetic sun, it nothing does: even its lovely light is borrowed.

Suddenly – *clang . . . clang . . . clang . . . clang . . . clang*: the Gas Alarm from the front trench. Someone in my platoon had seen a cloud of gas blowing towards us across No-Man's-Land. The wind bloweth where it listeth, no human being orders its direction or its strength; a gentle breeze travels several yards per second, the approaching cloud was probably already over the front trench, impossible to dodge it or take cover now. And this gentle breeze was burdened with yellowish-green phosgene gas. I saw the cloud approaching wishy-washy with stray wisps reaching up skywards, getting thicker every tenth part of a second till it became a dense cloud. Before I was wrapped in the deadly embrace, the innocent moon shone no more.

The completeness of this man-made eclipse appalled me. When we wake from a dream, or nightmare, the memory is usually disjointed, nonsense, which soon melts to nothing. My memory of my third night in trenches is like that, vivid in some detail, but in general a masterpiece of confusion.

When my mask was on I gasped, trying to control my breathing. I couldn't see through misted eyepieces, but I could hear – a rather muffled sound of rifle-fire from the front trench. Duty took charge of me. I must get to my platoon.

I felt my way along the side of the short communication trench, my breathing no longer difficult and the eyepieces

gradually getting clearer. Blast from a shrapnel shell momentarily blew a gap in the gas cloud, and I saw several men
(unrecognisable of course in their masks) standing irresolute as
though uncertain of purpose – all but one who made his
purpose apparent. He was without a mask, his head bare, his
white face expressing horror. Before the cloud of gas re-formed
I saw this man lurch sideways, arms outstretched, attempting
to pull off another man's mask; a third man, wielding what I
judged to be a bit of broken duckboard, pressed between the
two. I saw one of them fall to the ground. All over in a moment,
a vivid picture in my mind for ever and ever and ever.

Hours later, when the wind was pure again, the moon
shining over some distant land, I was told varied rumours
about this small tragedy – the hapless man never had a mask,
wasn't present when they were issued, or had lost it, or didn't
pin it to his shirt in the correct position, or in his fumbling let it
fall to the ground: undoubtedly he ran amok, till he collapsed
from breathing gas, or was knocked on the head by a comrade,
or perhaps was shot by an officer. Well, rumour is generous,
and in trenches Death is common: we manage without
coroners, or their inquests. When a man is dead from whatever cause he has finished with Life, what need is there to say
more? Doubtless his *name* liveth, on a war memorial in some
village, or maybe, a town hall, or a factory, or a church.

I was distracted by the horror I had witnessed. The Little
Willie shell near Poperinghe had shown me that I was no hero
and now, as I stumped on towards my men in the front trench, I
reflected that I faced another incontestible enemy – poison gas.

In the front trench I saw, within the short range of visibility,
hooded figures, side by side, firing as fast as they could load and
re-load, firing into the gas cloud coming across No-Man's-
Land. Completely useless. If the Bosche intended a raid or
attack in force, he couldn't do so till the gas was blown away. I

must stop this useless waste of ammunition, but how?

I saw huddled bodies, unconscious, down on duckboards in the trench; some who had torn off gas masks were coughing to death. Several times I noticed men, hands over their chests or clutching their heads, staggering away as casualties. I just didn't know what to do. I needed Sergeant Hill, but couldn't recognise him, couldn't tell one man from another. I went from man to man shouting at them through my mask to stop firing until they could *see* the enemy. At the same time I tried to space men better, where casualties left considerable gaps. While I was doing this I suddenly recognised Hill engaged in the same way. He shouted, 'Thank God you're all right, sir.'

Notwithstanding the noise of machine gun fire and shells, Sergeant Hill and I managed to confer. Encouraged by his presence I made suggestions – to bring up ammunition to the fire step from reserve so no man would be short if the enemy attacked when the gas was blown away; that the rations just brought up by the ration party should be protected from phosgene contamination; that every man must remain on the fire step till daylight at Dawn-Stand-To.

I had been confused to discover that every aspect of the front line was so unlike anything I expected, but this gas attack on my third day was confusion's masterpiece. Doubtless I left undone things which ought to have been done, but I was thrilled when Sergeant Hill said, 'You've done well, sir, couldn't have done it better if you'd been out a month, sir.'

Time doesn't exist in a crisis and I've no notion of how long it was before I saw the dirty white cloud around us getting thinner. I started to lift the edge of my mask to sniff the air but Hill, seeing my intention, grabbed my hand, 'Not yet, sir, wait till it's quite clear.' Just as well, for the gas came in three separate waves with two short intervals. At last I saw dimly through the smudged eyepieces of my mask a faint round moon;

the innocent moon, looking a little 'partworn' (to use a quarter-master's term).

Sergeant Hill and I were on duty continuously, busy with one thing or another. After the gas had all gone, the air pure again, some men suffered wracking coughs and staggered off to Casualty Clearing for treatment. Hill and I both had sore throats and slight headaches, nothing worse.

Hardy turned up during Stand-To, touring the company to assess our losses. 'God Almighty!' he exclaimed in a typical outburst, 'dead rats everywhere! In dug-outs . . . under duck-boards . . . on the fire step . . . and one there caught in the act, his head stuck in a Maconochie tin.' He gave a little laugh. 'Hundreds of the brutes, stiff as pokers, can't be one left alive . . . 'tis an ill wind that blows nobody any good, and an ill gas attack that doesn't rid you of rats!' Turning directly to me he said, '*Manual of Military Hygiene* no help in a show like this. You'd better put on a fatigue party – a few men to collect the corpses and fling 'em as far as possible over the parapet to rot in No-Man's-Land. They'll stink for a month. I was taught in Sunday School, count your blessings, count them one by one, but to lose all your rats in one night has a disadvantage; no one else comes round to trenches to empty dustbins or take away garbage.'

During the morning Sergeant Hill started to cough. As the paroxysms became worse I sent him to Casualty Clearing thinking the MO would have some suitable medicine. He was reluctant to go, but I think he knew better than I what to expect. By Dusk-Stand-To he was dead.

Hardy brought me the news. 'A damned awful night,' he added. 'Lucky you had Hill with you, but you passed the test all right.' I hardly heard this remark, my mind thinking of Sergeant Hill's death – a new degree of death to me, someone I'd been working alongside, a man who thought with me and for me, on whom I depended.

My platoon lost 31 men and I learned the battalion had 140 casualties, including 8 officers. Before the attack I was an ignoramus, now Hardy said I'd passed the test, whatever that meant. I had an experience behind me, awful to think about but a rare experience. From what Hardy said and from what other officers and the men told me, none of them had been in a cloud gas attack before. My self-confidence, which suffered so much on my way to Shrapnel Corner, was restored. I had survived what Hardy called 'a damned awful night'. Now he said, 'If the enemy come over before we are relieved by another battalion we have not enough men to stop them. You can bet the Staff have no prepared second line of defence this side of Calais,' a characteristic outburst.

During the night, while we were being relieved, the wind changed direction, blowing now south-west across No-Man's-Land towards the Bosche. Hardy said, 'Not quite as strong as we'd like but it's nice to know God is back on our side.' Later in the day when we were installed in reserve trenches he gave me an order. 'Sorry, Old Man, a working party for you tonight; no one else to send, can't go myself. You take twenty men to Hellfire Corner where a guide awaits you. Pick up gas cylinders, two men to each, take them to prepared places in front line trench called Ignorance Row, near Hooge. Some consolation, getting a bit of our own back, *an eye for an eye and a tooth for a tooth*, as God declared the Law to Moses.' He laughed, his words evident mockery: my mind was trying to grasp that I was being ordered to take part in a gas attack on the Germans and I had not known that we used this barbarous weapon at all. Hardy's mention of the old Jewish law and the fact that our gas attacks seemed to have been going on for months without any public mention of the old Jewish Law and the fact that our gas attacks 'Suppose it's all right.'

This was, I believe, the last time gas was used in clouds. It caused many casualties but could not be used on a wide enough front to be of strategic importance. A few weeks later the Germans started gas shells, which I found alarming and disruptive but not very effective.

Mark Hardy and I shared Life together for the next three weeks in conditions wholly strange to me. His influence nudged me, one way or the other, in all manner of decisions made during the rest of my life. His 'outbursts' (as I thought them) against military leaders astonished and at least half convinced me, but when I came to know him better I discovered an even more astonishing side of his character – as though I read a book and after a rather wordy chapter or two came to the main plot and from then on couldn't put it down. I respected him in part because he had experience of adult life between school and army which I had not. Naturally I wondered what he had done during those few significant years.

'What was I doing before the war?' Hardy repeated my question thoughtfully, as if it took time to recollect events of so long ago. 'I was at a parson-factory.'

'Golly! What's that?'

'Place where they manufacture parsons, of course. My pater is a clergyman, rector of a parish near Hereford . . . brought me up to follow in his footsteps, sent me to a church school – a lousy hole! Then to this parson-factory in Cambridge. Don't look so moonstruck, place was chocablock with would-be Reverends.'

Now I understood a remark he made on the morning after the gas attack, 'Hell of a night for you . . . what Napoleon called a Baptism of Fire . . . not just a sprinkling . . . what the Baptists call total immersion, in at the deep end, so to speak.' I'd been surprised at any reference to religion and especially to Baptists; what the army called one of the 'fancy religions'.

'If you'd told me you spent a few years going to the moon

with HG Wells I should know you were kidding, but . . .' He interrupted me with a laugh.

'Soon as war came I escaped, bolted to a recruiting office and took the King's shilling. All the pater could do then was chivvy some fellow with influence to get me a commission . . . and here I am.'

'You'll go back to Cambridge after the war?' (I surprised myself using the phrase after-the-war. We spoke usually of 'the duration', implying a very distant date, which we as individuals would be lucky to attain.)

Hardy answered my question with one word – 'disillu-sioned.'

After an impressive pause he recited a verse from a poem new to me, Fitz Gerald's translation of *The Rubaiyat of Omar Khayyam*:

> Myself when young did eagerly frequent
> Doctor and Saint, and heard great Argument
> About it and about: but evermore
> Came out by the same Door as in I went.

Disillusion was, presumably, the realisation that what seemed to be the truth was false. Hardy was not alone. *The New Church Times*, a trench newspaper published by some Sherwood Foresters from a dug-out under the remains of a village in the Salient named Neuve-Eglise, contained comic advertisments; one claimed a

> Cure for OPTIMISM, do you think all is going well for the allies? Do you think the war will end within 12 months? Do you consider our Leaders are competent? If your answer to any of these questions is 'Yes', then you have the dread disease OPTIMISM and we can cure you.

This was not anti-war sentiment, quite the reverse, but certain-ly the beginning of disillusion.

Hardy's particular target was the teaching of the Church.

Theology at my parson-factory was a rag-bag of ancient doctrines invented by men who knew only one part of the world, lived in a civilisation which has passed away . . . Christianity, the most important influence in the thousands of years of *homo sapiens*, is not the only influence. Our church leaders are intolerant, claim to decide what Christians must believe. Fact is they know precious little about men. Do 'em good to spend a few weeks in trenches experiencing the reality of life. The Church has drifted away from Jesus, become materialist and class-conscious. Its true we sing the *Magnificat* (a great revolutionary song) but the Litany and Morning and Evening prayers ought to include The Beatitudes of Jesus. We pay homage to the élite in society – to royalty, magistrates, members of parliament and all in Authority, but we've cut out the Poor in Spirit, the Meek, the Merciful and the Peacemakers.

Such observations were typical. We had opportunites for confidential talks now we were the only officers in D Company. I was not surprised that Hardy, so practical as a company commander, so realistic, had definite plans for after the war. No return to the parson-factory, but social work involving politics based especially on his experience with our men. One day as we chatted in a candle-lit dug-out in Sanctuary Wood, he surprised me. 'What about you?' he asked. 'What will you do if we ever get out of this?' Of course, I had ambitions; at school most of us in the top forms had planned professional careers – law, medicine, the church, teaching, commerce – but we'd put them quite out of mind for the war. Before I could answer, a thud, a thunderclap explosion made all creation shudder. When the vibration ceased a thin stream of dried earth began to cascade from a split sandbag in the dug-out roof. Hardy made for the entrance saying, 'better look at the damage above.' I intended to follow but was fascinated to watch the slow but steady increase in size of the earth cataract. In time the sandbag would be empty – could be the beginning of the end of our dug-out shelter.

Blast from a second mortar threw Hardy four or five yards against a bit of old railway line used to strengthen the traverse of our trench. The stretcher-bearers reckoned half his bones were broken and came back from Casualty Clearing saying the MO reported, 'concussion and severe multiple wounds'. Always difficult to get news of a man who went down wounded: eventually I had a card from 2nd Eastern General Hospital, Brighton, 'Time *you* got a Blighty, can recommend this place except for too much Jippo, expect to be here for duration.' Fourteen months later I saw Mark Hardy again for a few minutes, then no more. He still haunts my mind like a familiar ghost in an old house.

At school we dared one another to do risky or dangerous things. In trenches so much was strange, unexpected, unimagined, that I often made impetuous decisions; dared myself, so to speak, without considering what might be involved.

I hadn't been out very long when two brother-officers told me they were going to visit a recently opened army canteen. Would I come too? I didn't know where this canteen was but gladly accepted the friendly suggestion. The battalion was out of trenches in Reserve. To my surprise my friends took me to the Transport Officer, 'to get horses' they explained. I discovered we were to ride to the village with the canteen, twelve kilometres away. Both my friends were accustomed to riding, one being a hunting man who sometimes talked of his pre-war hunting exploits. I knew nothing of horses. When at boarding school in London I'd been thrilled to see London Fire Brigade horses charging along a street with a fire engine and I used to watch staid horses drawing tram cars slowly along Green Lanes, near Finsbury Park, but that's as near as I'd ever been to a horse. I looked at the huge animal brought out for me by the Transport Officer and wondered how to get abroad. I watched my friends mount – without a ladder, and then confessed I'd never ridden. 'Golly,' said the hunting man, 'never been on a horse.' He spoke as though this accomplishment came naturally in childhood as does speech. The other chap laughed at my apprehension. 'Everything has a first time, Old Man. You'll be all right, we're not riding across open country, all the way alongside the road on the unpaved part.' Somehow I got astride that creature and looked down to the ground far far below.

All went well – at first: no traffic on the road, no other riders. Then we came to a long straight part of the road and the hunting man proposed a canter, perhaps a gallop. He said to me, 'You keep at a walk, we'll wait for you outside the canteen.' I don't think my horse heard. I was comfortably astride, knees pressed into the creature's flanks, reins firmly in my hands, but the Transport Officer was no doubt correct when he said our horses were 'fresh'. Mine may have been a bit slow in the uptake, anyway when the others broke into a trot he began to prance so that I almost went overboard on one side and, struggling to get the centre of gravity, nearly slithered off the other flank. For a few moments I had little control but I tugged at the reins and shouted 'Whoa' (which I had heard drivers of cabs and carts cry and which I supposed must be understood by an intelligent hunting horse). But he was ambitious: could see the others ahead and getting further away every minute; if this were a race he wasn't going to be an also-ran. To be fair I don't think he had any animus towards me personally. I doubt if he gave me a thought. We trotted and, I believe, cantered. All I can claim is I kept my seat – well, perhaps, kept aboard. A turn in the road and the others were out of sight: not that it mattered to me for my spectacles fell off my nose. Luckily they were the pince-nez type with a thin gold chain to one ear so they weren't smashed but just swung about my face, to and fro, as if looking for a pair of short-sighted eyes to adopt. It would be an exaggeration to say I lost all control over the horse for I don't think I ever really had any.

I'm sure we cantered round that turning in the road. I could see well enough to make out the others now a long way ahead, but I also saw to my consternation a large company of soldiers, fallen out for a halt, on the left side of the road, sitting on the bank or lying on the edge of the road. Colonials obviously, Canadians I guessed. They probably lived on horseback at home, had watched the others ride by and saw I was no equestrian. A runaway horse out of control! They shouted, jumped up, ran across the road to intercept, but my horse was probably now firmly convinced we were in the Grand National. We swept beyond them to loud cheers. I daresay we were half a kilometre from the canteen when my companions reined in a little, slowed to a trot. Not my horse: we came up at a gallop, no pilgrim pace for us. The path narrowed a fraction but he swept past the others, which I admit was taking an unfair advantage. Unfortunately he swept a little too close to the hunting man's horse which stumbled and nearly threw its rider. I wasn't prepared for the contempt and bitter remarks of my friends. The hunting man never forgave me, wouldn't respond to my apology.

That was my first horse ride – twenty-four kilometres there and back: but not my last. Once I rode alone forty-two kilometres to collect money for the battalion from an Army Pay Office. When I came from the office with rather a heavy bag of coins I thought I should never be able to mount, the horse thought so too. At every attempt he started homewards before I was astride. Luckily a lance-corporal, watching from the Pay Office window, came out and held the horse's head and the money bag while I climbed awkwardly into the saddle. Jobs of which I had no previous experience or knowledge and no one to advise me, had to be tackled willy-nilly, occasionally dared.

CHAPTER FIVE

No-Man's-Land

After Hardy went down wounded I was the only officer in D Company. The Adjutant told me more officers were expected daily, but till then I was temporarily in command. 'Manage as best you can,' he said. 'If in doubt ask Captain Fitch of C Company. I've told him to keep an eye on you.'

Amongst papers I found in Company HQ a recent order puzzled me – *Company Commanders are prohibited from going beyond the front line trench.* The front line *is* the front line, the ultimate limit. How could anyone go beyond? While I puzzled over this, another order came – *Junior Officers intending to patrol in No-Man's-Land must notify a Company Commander of their intention.* Evidently 'beyond the front line' meant No-Man's-Land.

No-Man's-Land, a romantic name for the strip of waste land between the armies, once growing crops for human food or grazing cattle and sheep, now empty land, devoid of life, save only rats and small vermin, the very earth churned up by shells and mortar fire so that even common weeds seem reluctant to risk their sturdy lives in such a place! A wilderness no one would give a song for, not *Tipperary* or *There's a long long trail a-winding.* Literally no *man's* land, no longer belonging to any human being (presumably 'No Man' is God, the creator of all the world, who else could he be?). Empty land, a boundary such as children imagine Tom Tiddler's Ground; a neutral corridor stretching twistingly from North Sea to Alps, varying in width from a few yards to hundreds, in all a few thousand acres of Mother Earth which her children do not seem to want; used only to keep armies apart, rather as adults separate squabbling schoolboys so they don't actually fight.

Had I interpreted these rather flabby orders correctly? I consulted Captain Fitch. 'Panic orders,' he commented with a laugh. 'Someone at the War Office or in War Cabinet has discovered too many of us getting killed, compared with other ranks. For my part I'm damned glad of any order which positively bans *me* from crawling about in No-Man's-Land. Some sense in patrols when the Front was less defined than now. Officers used to patrol to keep a check on enemy positions – machine gun emplacements, listening posts and so on. I reckon that game is played out, not worth the candle, as gamblers say.'

'What is it like to be in No-Man's-Land?'

'Tense . . . total exposure . . . no trench to give you any protection . . . soon as you go beyond our barbed wire you crawl, flat on stomach, moving towards the Bosche front line, inches at a time, every sense alert.'

He described in detail this ultimate experience for PBI subaltern officers: eyes searching the shadows for sight of any enemy patrol, ears listening till they seemed to stick out from your head a yard each side, fingers feeling the ground ahead to avoid unbalancing stones with your next crawl, even the lesser senses like smell were important – Jerry's cooking, or the stench of a latrine indicating the proximity of a front line, or the distinct smell of rotting flesh as the first warning of a corpse. And darkness your only protection, darkness that couldn't stop a bullet. Darkness which every now and then was ruptured by a Very-Light. Until that had expended itself the slightest movement was fatal, your only protection is immobility, freezing every muscle in your body no matter how awkward. And always at any time, moonlight or pitch dark, machine gun fire might sweep across No-Man's-Land on the odd chance of catching a victim, sending bullets close enough to comb your hair.

'And you are now banned this pleasure, sir,' I said, trying to imagine the conditions he described, 'How do I know when I ought to patrol?'

He spoke kindly, 'No one is going to *order* you to go into No-Man's-Land. This second order makes it clear it's up to you to decide if and when you do. Forget it; at any rate till you are thoroughly familiar with all the routine and everyday responsibilities of trench life. That'll take a few weeks; and, who knows, you may get a Blighty!' He concluded, 'No one here takes much notice of orders which drift down on us from remote HQ.'

I took this advice, threw myself into immediate duties; only climbed at night out of the front trench, over the parapet, to spend a few minutes examining and repairing our barbed wire, but I didn't go beyond into the real No-Man's-Land. Not that I ceased to think of it. Captain Fitch's description refused to be forgotten, like a bad thought which conscience tells you should be forgotten, but can't. The very words he used echoed in my mind frequently, nagged at me till they became a challenge; and No-Man's-Land was a challenge which scared me.

Most days we had casualties from shells or mortars. I watched men die, angry that I hadn't been trained what to do before stretcher-bearers could turn up. Sometimes I helped to bury the dead, all I felt competent to do; a necessary procedure between Life and Death which some clergmen invest with imagined importance. Like all PBI in the front trench, I shrank into myself a little whenever I heard a shell coming my way. I didn't fear death but life is so familiar. I feared only the agony I saw others suffer.

I don't usually dither when in doubt, more likely to act precipitately. One day I told my Company Commander I intended to go on patrol, no date or purpose mentioned; it was for me to decide, my initiative, but I rather hoped he would discourage me. All he said was, 'Up to you, Old Man.' Next day, Chance (in the form of a 5.9 shell) considerably damaged our parapet. My sergeant said he could now see down a ridge running across No-Man's-Land. 'Looks like a corpse out there, sir. Reckon Jerry can't see it, been there probably since the raid they made on the West Kents.'

'Might interest our Intelligence,' I observed. 'I'll patrol after the moon is down, and . . . have . . . a look . . . at him.' The last hesitant words sounded like a hammer driving in nails. I ought to have taken one or two reliable men with me on patrol, but I was answering a personal challenge, my initiative, (identifying the corpse only an excuse). I didn't like to involve others. Moving in No-Man's-Land was more difficult than I expected; crawling at snail's pace over irregular shell holes I lost sense of direction, couldn't find the corpse, often didn't know if I were going towards the enemy front line, or back to ours. The tension was terrific, building up within me to near breaking point. I suppose I'd been creeping about for more than an hour watching, listening, and hiding my face in putrid earth when a Very Light landed almost on top of me. It couldn't have been as close as I thought or its final flare would have burned me, but I looked up and saw that I was only a few yards from the enemy front trench. Worse – a man was staring straight at me. I had a clear impression of him, nice-looking chap, square face, high forehead, flat cheeks, very prominent chin, and fair hair like a girl – unmistakeably German – but why no helmet? He uttered a kind of half-suppressed cry of alarm and backed away from the rapidly diminishing light.

How I got back I don't know, stood up and ran for it, expecting every moment to be shot. Challenged by one of our sentries I gave the night's password and dropped back into our front line with more than a feeling of relief. I was elated. My batman was there with hot cocoa, and the men who came round me looked on me, I thought, with a kind of admiration.

My first patrol in No-Man's-Land, and the fleeting encounter with a German made me realise an extraordinary fact which hadn't dawned on me before. I had actually *seen* a living German, the first one in the three months I'd been out. We not only fight against ineluctable forces, we fight invisible enemies.

An invisible enemy: did other PBI Subalterns serving in the front line get a like impression? I do not know. The first mention in my diary of seeing the enemy is dated three months and two days after I arrived in France – all *dead* Germans, killed a few days before by artillery fire when the Bosche had to abandon a trench. The first *living* enemy I saw were machine gunners who decimated us as we attempted to advance in daylight during the Somme battle, mowed us down before we had covered fifteen yards.

Looking back now over the whole of my experience at the Front I detect a pattern not discernible at the time. The trench line was established in 1914 when the BEF dug themselves in to withstand attacks by the German army. I could not know that this line would remain almost unchanged until March 1918: the three great battles, Verdun, Somme and Passchendaele (in two of which I was to perform a small part) were unsuccessful attempts to get back to conventional open warfare.

Someone has described trench life as long periods of intense boredom interspersed with moments of acute fear; my friend Hardy spoke of the front line as a prison from which the only escape is as a casualty; and years ago the poet Browning coined the phrase, 'our wearisome pedantic war'. I now recognise the point in these views but I did not at the time. Maybe, coming from school to trenches I found everything so strange and exciting that I missed the dullness.

71

I recall something like a routine in trench life which was of course often disrupted. Usually we did a cycle of twenty-four days and nights – six in front trench, six in close support, another six in front trench then six in Rest. This cycle was repeated *ad infinitum*. Close support was in trenches about five hundred to a thousand yards behind the front line but always on alert, no undressing, no boots off, which meant a total of eighteen days with little chance of anything like a bodywash. Occasionally we suffered from lice, but a big advantage of close support was longer sleep than the cat-naps of the front line. Rest was usually in the ruins of a derelict village but more happily in isolated farm buildings still occupied by a farmer and his family. On Rest we could undress, get a good sleep, seldom heard a shell. Officers and perhaps a few men sometimes managed a day-trip to an occupied town or village right out of the war area.

Although the enemy was invisible we seldom had a day or night without casualties. Death did not appal me, though I was sickened by the sight of mutilated bodies, entrails torn out, a mass of flesh, blood and clothing which somehow could never add up to one human being. Death, I reassured myself, is only the end of Life. What troubled me, more than words can tell, were the wounded. I had no idea how to cope; stretcher-bearers not always immediately available and the poor chaps couldn't be moved in daylight. A young man screaming in agony goes on screaming in your mind long after you've buried him.

The shortage of officers was met temporarily by subalterns from our second battalion; in India since the war began. Apart from making periods on duty shorter, they were a welcome addition to the Company Mess; instead of eating alone or sharing a meal with one other we were now sometimes four or five. The fellows from India came talking of polo and tiger hunting with Maharajas. They were Sandhurst-trained professionals, but as ignorant of war as I had been when I came from Blighty. We teased them, called them Pukka Sahibs. One, christened by us Rajah because of an injudicious remark about living with an Indian prince, was a splendid raconteur; story after story of Asian life carried our thoughts away from the Front and showed me, if not the others, that the real world is bigger than a school atlas.

The short friendships of trench life encourage tolerance. With no confident expectation of being alive tomorrow one easily accepts the right of every individual to an opinion and personal habits. But it wasn't only Pukka Sahibs who drew upon our tolerance. We had other eccentrics. One awkward fellow (a farmer from a village near Ilkley, chap with a pretentious name which we shortened to Spud) was frugal, austere and spoke seldom except to condemn our rather frequent grumbling about insufficient sleep. Spud would throw at us a north country saying, 'Six hours for a man, seven for a woman, eight for a fool.' Once when I added 'and two hours for PBI in front line,' he turned on me savagely: 'What you long for is a Blighty with six months in a hospital bed or maybe fifty years on your back at that place for men who've lost all their limbs.' A strange character, Spud. Someone had a parcel from home with a cake, as usual shared by the Mess. Spud took his slice and threw it into No-Man's-Land muttering something about officers feeding better than the men. We were furious; but much later, when I'd been out a year and learned the satisfaction which comes from total sharing, I wondered if perhaps Spud had been right.

A very different character who gave us something to laugh about was Clarence Joy. When asked what he did in his civilian capacity he was so evasive that we concluded he had something to hide, not really wicked, just a bit shady. Joy had a cheerful habit of singing softly to himself when he thought he was unobserved, sentimental ditties like the *Indian Love Lyrics*. 'Must be in love,' was one obvious surmise, 'dreaming of a girl in Blighty.' One of the Pukka Sahibs offered another explanation, 'Fellow who sings so out of tune when the Mess is out of whisky must have a serious vice – probably opium, lots of addicts in India.'

When Joy was not in the Mess we invented likely occupations for him – doctor with cheerful bedside manner, a Bishop's Chaplain, or an important lay official in an ecclesiastical organisation. Could he be a clerk in some charity, giving him the necessary social contacts when he applied for a commission? Our guesses were all wrong. The truth came out one night when the Post Clerk handed us our letters – a batch of seventeen for Joy, all in like envelopes. To have so many was slightly embarrassing, calling for comment. Joy confessed shamefacedly that all were Birthday Cards from schoolgirls. So that was Clarence Joy's shady past before he became a soldier – taught in a *girls'* school!

It wasn't only in the Officers' Mess that attempts were made to counteract the grimness of our prison life. On every possible occasion the men turned to sport. We had Inter-Platoon matches and Inter-Company Championships, football most of the year, in summer cricket. We played in any weather, on any condition of ground where we happened to be and at all available times: for instance a match between my company and B Company only a few hours before we started a night trek to relieve a battalion of Warwicks in the front line. I wrote the score on the back of a trench map; we won 3–0, and I added, below, the names of two officers killed and three wounded during the relief.

Everyone has heard of the rival armies fraternising in No-Man's-Land at Christmas 1914, English and Germans leaving their trenches to talk together and kick a football around. By

1916 conditions were very different. I wrote on Christmas Eve, 'Big strafe, lots of *minnies* and *pineapples* (enemy trench mortars), general alarm, expected start of Big Push.' War had become more serious and we assumed the fraternising stories to be only sentimental yarns. How do you fraternise without a common language? None of my men and none of the officers knew any German, but communication doesn't always depend on the spoken word. It was probably the football that allowed the fraternising in 1914.

Every day (in hours of light and dark) we had casualties, almost all from long-range enemy artillery, batteries out of sight, we an immovable target. When a strafe was on us we damned all Germans, but when our RA was pounding the enemy front line, our chaps would say, 'Poor buggers across there copping it.'

I don't know if these sentiments and judgements of the front line were shared generally by units serving outside the fighting area. Our isolation undoubtedly aggravated our pride – we PBI were the chaps who mattered, the ones who bore the brunt of war, obviously indispensible; though, to be sure, there *were* other branches of the army. Not that we saw much of them; occasionally an RA observer, occasionally a chaplain, almost never our MO (probably overworked with casualties brought down by stretcher-bearers). Not that we *wanted* visitors, just the opposite; caught in a strafe or an enemy raid or a general attack visitors would have been a proper menace. For my part I was always conscious that I had sole responsibility for my tiny little bit of the Western Front, I and I alone was arbiter there. While this proud feeling was upon me a very surprising event made me the laughing stock of the battalion, indeed of the whole brigade. I was visited one morning by a General.

The chap must be dead now but I won't disclose his name: he was well-known in military circles, doubtless left descendants, some of whom might not appreciate the comic aspect of this incident. 'Tell no absurdity of the dead' is perhaps more important than 'speak no evil'.

I am careful to avoid any exaggeration. I was on duty in the front line at Dead Horse Corner, just north of Piccadilly Circus in the Bois de Ploegsteert (Plugstreet to our men), a comparatively quiet sector.

My sergeant, running round a traverse, reported breathlessly, 'Sir, two men coming down Broadway (a communication trench), one is a General.' Before I could grasp this extraordinary news, the General was with me, demanding, 'Am I in the front line?' and, before I could answer, 'Are you the officer in charge?' He seemed an old man, certainly over thirty, with a severe face, as though he had never found anything to laugh at since he was a child. His eyes, under heavy eyebrows, looked downwards distrustingly. With him was a Staff Officer, a decent sort, I thought. He nodded to me reassuringly.

'I am in *command* of this area, sir.' I hoped the General would realise from my abrupt, rather dignified reply that even in his august presence I was responsible for whatever happened here. Looking about him the General asked, 'What's that thing on a stick?'

'Trench mirror, sir, to look across No-Man's-Land.'

'Not big enough; you ought to have proper box periscopes.' Turning to the Staff Officer he said, 'Make a note of it.'

I ventured to expostulate, 'These small mirrors allow quite a clear view across to the enemy trenches, sir. If you will stand just here you will see.' While he was looking the Staff Officer whispered to me, 'Sorry I couldn't warn you of our visit. The old boy decided quite suddenly he wanted to see a trench.'

'Better than I expected,' admitted the General, 'but I'll order box periscopes to be issued to you. Military Outfitters in

76

London sell them, no reason why you men out here shouldn't have the best.'

'Little mirrors have advantages, sir,' I insisted. 'They withstand shell blast which would crack anything larger and the protecting flap keeps off the rain.'

Ignoring my comment he said, 'I saw through your mirror what looked like wooden stakes just over the parapet. Why are they lying out there?'

'Last night a shell dropped in our wire. Tonight I shall take four men before moon-rise to repair the damage, sir. The stakes have been thrown out ready for the job.'

'Won't staked wire impede you when you go over the top?'

I recalled Hardy's words. Was this old Dug-Out dreaming of fifteen years ago in South Africa? And then suddenly a very-much-alive thought struck me. Was there something the General knew which I didn't? Rumours told of fighting down south somewhere on the Somme . . . vague reports . . . the Big Push perhaps . . . hinting at open fighting . . . had he come to see what trenches were like because he expected we might be involved in a Big Push from Plugstreet? Was he not such an old Dug-Out as he seemed? Was I the simpleton? Anyway, I'd had enough of him in my command. I showed him our Lewis Gun section, and where I sited two small trench mortars, and then said firmly, 'That's about all, sir.'

'Very interesting . . . very interesting,' he said. 'Your dispositions are satisfactory.' He stood looking at me from his down-looking eyes as though something more ought to be said.

'Would you like a guide to take you to battalion headquarters, sir?'

'No, no,' he said, and the Staff chap said airily, 'I know the way.'

My sergeant stood with me watching them negotiate a

rickety patch of duckboard. 'First time I've seen a General in the front line,' I observed.

'Like a dream, sir . . . can't hardly believe it.'

For me it wasn't the last of the General, though I never saw him again. Half an hour later the Adjutant turned up.

'Suppose you are the young officer who showed the General round?'

'Yes, sir. First time I've encountered a real live General.'

'Well, he made a complaint about you.'

'Complaint?' I was astonished, and for a second or two rather dismayed. 'He seemed to approve everything, sir, spoke about satisfactory dispositions.'

'Oh! Not that kind of complaint. Said you explained everything very well. He described you as an intelligent young officer. His complaint is that you wear earrings.'

'Earrings? Did you say earrings? Some sort of joke, sir?'

He nodded. 'The CO and I were amazed, thought better of you! We asked him to repeat the word. He was definite – indeed, ordered the CO to make sure the practice of wearing earrings is stopped forthwith.' The Adjutant spoke quite seriously, giving me time to gather some thoughts, then he grinned. 'The CO guessed the riddle – the little chain from your pince-nez spectacles which fits round your ear!' A very ordinary device in common use sold by opticians everywhere, worn by many thousands, to save glasses from being broken if they fall off or are knocked off – especially desirable in trenches to withstand the blast from shells or mortars. Earrings! It had to be a joke.

'What brought the General here, sir? Must have been something special.'

'God knows.'

'Who is he, sir?'

'Our corps commander – God help us!'

In no time my earrings were the talk of the battalion, one of those jokes too good to be true. But it was true. Two days later Divisional Orders had a paragraph, 'The attention of all officers is called to King's Regulations, page 193, item D – officers not allowed to wear jewellery when in uniform.' The following day the same warning appeared in Brigade Orders, quoting Divisional Orders; and yet a third time, a day later, in Battalion Orders quoting Brigade Orders.

Hardly credible? It was the only time I saw a General in the front line.

Waking reluctantly one day I overheard a conversation between my batman, Tidmarsh, and a chap who'd just come out from Blighty: the newcomer, attracted by the smell of a meal Tidmarsh was cooking for me, grumbled that officers evidently had better rations than the rank and file. My batman explained he was cooking some tinned concoction from a shop still open in a derelict village, bought and paid for by the Officers' Mess. Tidmarsh added, 'This stuff is not much more than a flavour. Officers have the same rations as you and me and anyway my officer is used to better grub at home than us . . . it's hard for them to miss what they've always had.'

In fact we did supplement rations when we could, extras like sardines and tinned fruits – pears, apricots, peaches, pineapple chunks. Otherwise we ate exactly the same rations as the men, brought up usually at night by a Ration Party. Of course they didn't always reach the front line. I remember living once for nearly three weeks on bully beef and biscuits (hard, square, half-inch thick, as sold for very large dogs) and jam (always plum and apple in the army). Not starvation, but tedious. Tidmarsh said one morning, 'found a fifty-pound crate of biscuits, sir, so I broke into it, so they'll be fresh today . . . sort of . . .'

Officers took turns to buy the supplementaries, as and when possible, sharing the cost. At one time we had in the Mess a snob called Joseph, always talking of his superior social status, an aristocrat who couldn't descend to middle-class practices even at the Front. 'All very well for you fellows to go shopping,' he would say, 'I wasn't brought up to it.' He made such remarks frankly, with good-humour and authority as though all the world must accept his standards. We were rather amused, laughed at his self-importance and conceded him immunity.

Once he came with me to a shop kept open by a French woman who was making a fortune out of English soldiers. While I bought the usual tinned fruit Joseph wandered round looking at the shelves. Suddenly he cried, 'Look, see all those tins, Old Man, that really *is* a luxury. I forget the name, it's like caviare but richer, without the slight fishy flavour, a rare delicacy, only get it in London at shops like Harrods who stock imported specialities. It's got a French name . . . you must know it.' I didn't, but then caviare was no more than a name to me, never tasted it, never seen it in the larder at home.

'We must buy some tins of that,' said Joseph, 'about twenty tins on the shelf, old stock, pre-war I reckon but those delicacies keep well. We'd better take the lot before someone else spots them. We could eat a tin at a meal, would transform our rations.' He went on talking enthusiastically – recalling Country House parties where they had served it and once at a Lord Mayor's banquet. I didn't think he was serious, never considered anything said by Joseph as serious, but I looked at a tin. The printed wording on it was French, some sort of instructions about cooking I imagined, but most was illegible, faded or covered by dust. A few large letters were readable (part of the name Joseph couldn't remember I thought). I left him and continued my shopping of our usual extras and when

I returned he was rubbing his hands in pleasure. He had done a deal (as he expressed it) with the French woman, buying twenty tins at a bargain price. 'Made her take off five sous from every tin because she admits they are covered in thick dust and grit from a recent shell in the Place Publique.' Joseph insisted that I paid because it was for the Mess account.

That evening, before our meal, Tidmarsh came to me with an open tin. 'Not sure how to serve this, sir. I think just spread a bit thick on toast but it has a sort of turpentine smell.' This was not altogether surprising because water was carried up to trenches in two-gallon petrol cans and was often tainted. Joseph at once said, 'The slight smell goes when it's heated, be sure the toast is really hot.' But the smell didn't go, the stuff tasted awful, uneatable. Next day I showed a tin to my friend the battalion Intelligence Officer. 'Something for you to exercise your intelligence on,' I muttered. He scrubbed the tin, put a few drops of petrol on the wording. 'The name ends with "que",' he said, 'and starts "E . . . N . . . C . . . A". We've a French dictionary at battalion HQ. I'll try to trace it.' Next day he reported, 'I reckon it is "encaustique". If so, what you have bought is twenty tins of beeswax furniture polish. You'll have to start looking around for some furniture for your dug-out.'

CHAPTER SIX

The Somme

The twin sisters Rumour and Superstition flourish in war. When war begins the immediate casualty is Truth, leaving a vacuum to be filled somehow. The ill-favoured sisters step in, become respectable, and are almost a psychological necessity. They spread and grow like weeds even as the beautiful red poppy weed of Flanders encroaches everywhere on cultivated crops.

Dominating the battlefields of the Somme is the town of Albert and dominating the little town is a cathedral; on the top of its tower is a gigantic figure of Virgin and Child. This statue was hit by a German shell, knocked sideways, to hang at ninety degrees, horizontally, face to the ground as though the Virgin couldn't bear to go on looking across the wide chalk downs with villages and woodlands being so rapidly destroyed by violent men. And a superstition arose which everyone who fought on the Somme wanted to believe – that when another shell chanced to hit the pendant statue, bringing the Virgin and Child crashing into the street below, the war would end. Nonsense, of course, impossible without a miracle, but men like us who lived alongside fear needed miracles. Such superstitions and rumours were always welcome in the restricted conversation of a small mess and, if a bit thin, could be nourished with a little imagination before being passed on to new-comers.

On our long trek southward to the Somme area we encountered regiments outside our own brigade, met officers in other branches of the army. During a few hours' halt in an inhabited

The Author at Southampton, 18 April 1916, about to sail for Le Havre

Officers' bayonet-fighting class, Guernsey, 1915. The Author is third from the right in the middle row. Potter, with whom he shared a tent, is second from left in the back row

The Author (standing). Taken behind the Ypres Salient some time
in 1916

Talbot House, Poperinghe,
Home of Toc H

Cartoon from *The New Church
Times*, a trench newspaper
published by some Sherwood
Foresters from a dug-out in
Neuve Eglise. "Amongst the
PBI, probably the best joke of
the war" (see P.130)

A soldier using a trench
mirror, a simple form of
periscope preferred by the
Author because it withstood
shell-blast

Bringing up bombs during the Battle of the Somme, July 1916.

One of the first tanks at Flers on the Somme, September 1916. It was here that the Author saw a tank for the only time during the war—possibly this one

Men of the North Staffs with captured German machine guns,
November 1916. "Our losses were mostly from cleverly concealed
machine guns, well sited to give overlapping fire."
"After the tank I think the most effective new weapon was the
Minenwerfer." A trench mortar with a range of 500 yards.

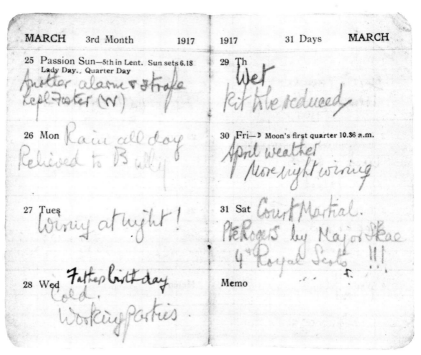

| MARCH | 3rd Month | 1917 | 1917 | 31 Days | MARCH |

25 Passion Sun—5th in Lent. Sun sets 6.18
Lady Day.. Quarter Day

Another alarm & strafe
Lcpl Foster (W)

26 Mon *Rain all day*
Relieved to Bully

27 Tues *Wiring at night!*

28 Wed *Father's birthday*
Cold.
Working Parties.

29 Th *Wet*
Kit Able reduced

30 Fri—☽ Moon's first quarter 10.36 a.m.
April weather
More night wiring

31 Sat *Court Martial.*
Pte Rogers by Major Skae
4th Royal Scots !!!

Memo

Pages from the Author's diary

Cleaning up after coming out of the trenches, near Ypres 1917

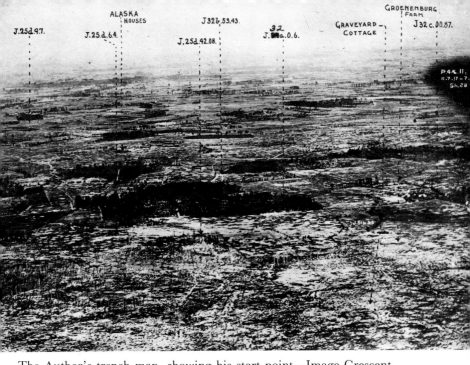

The Author's trench map, showing his start point—Image Crescent, his target—Jehovah Trench, and where he was hit—Graveyard Cottage, on the first day of the Battle of Passchendaele, 1917. Above, the first air-photo issued to the Author, of the same area. All trees in the trench area are destroyed but beyond the woods are undamaged.

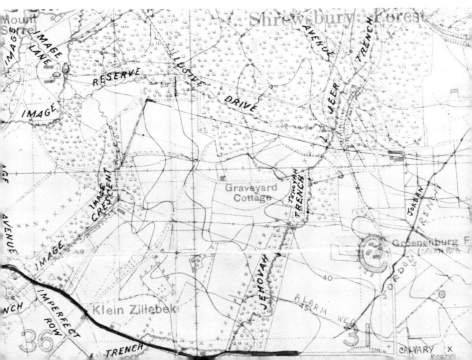

The Author's battalion on church parade, six weeks after he was wounded, September 1917. Evidently a special occasion since these were normally held around some building or ruins where men could relax. "I liked these parades, they were simple, no rituals or theology, only hymns, a lesson read from the Bible and a short address by the Chaplain."

Survivors of the Author's battalion, happy to be out of the line, September 1917

town I picked up a rumour from a chap in the Royal Artillery. I needed a haircut (a minor problem in trenches) and seeing the shop of a *Barbier* went in and gesticulated. A woman came forward, misunderstood my strange movements and told me in high-speed French that she would shave me. Pointing to a chair she produced a soapy brush and a cut-throat razor. It was a haircut I wanted but here was an experience not to be missed – shaved by a woman! The RA officer, sitting in the next chair having his hair cut by a boy laughed and said to me, 'Couldn't you find a woman in Blighty who'd cut your throat for you!' Afterwards we sat in a street café drinking coffee and he told me the latest rumour, speaking in a low voice with appropriate if rather theatrical caution. It was really a juicy rumour, but flavourless because he knew no details, nothing beyond the grand concept.

That evening I told my mess-mates. 'A new weapon . . . brand new . . . Bosche have always been ahead of us, first to use cloud-gas, first with flame-throwers, better aircraft than the Flying Corps, more guns than the RA, ten times more machine guns and we've only just caught up from the shell-shortage . . . that's past history. Now we've a new weapon; going to make history . . . a real breakthrough . . . end the war quickly.'

Some of my comrades listened cheerfully, discounting for exaggeration but acknowledging there might be something behind *any* rumour; others put sensible questions which I couldn't answer except to affirm, 'I don't know because this weapon is *really* new, never thought of before.' One said, 'They'll be wanting you, Old Man, at Army HQ to embroider official communiqués.' To be sure, I was acting. I knew no more than the RA chap told me and he only knew a rumour floating around.

A night came when, leading my men to a heavily contested position in the Somme battle, I heard above the sound of artillery fire strange noises from a wood that had not yet been entirely destroyed by shells. Although midsummer that night was exceptionally dark, lit only intermittently by flashes from firing guns. My sergeant said, 'Sounds like some kind of engine, sir.' 'Keep with the men,' I ordered, 'I'm going to investigate.' Very soon I was beyond the tree stumps, the ground irregular, the engine sounds close. Suddenly I realised the blackness ahead was solid, like a huge metal wall. My rumour . . . the new weapon! I hurried back to my men and as we moved towards our objective I exerted my imagination for the enlightenment of my sergeant.

'You were right about an engine . . . a great thing like one of those storage tanks for water on the roofs of big buildings, with an engine inside to propel it and I suppose men . . . a kind of land battleship.' As we walked on over ground made uneven by shell holes, branches of trees and stumps, I gave my thoughts absolute freedom, 'This new weapon will be irresistible, will cross No-Man's-Land, go over trenches, withstand small arms fire and machine gun fire, perhaps even field-gun shells . . . Jerry infantry will be helpless.'

The sergeant only half believed. 'First stop Berlin, sir?'

I recalled (as I often did) my feelings of utter helplessness over the Little Willie shell at Poperinghe. 'P'raps not Berlin tomorrow, sergeant, but this is more than a new weapon . . . could be a new *kind* of warfare.'

What I had seen was one of the first tanks, moving up to go into action at dawn. An official report a few days later claimed a great success, 'one of our tanks was seen in the main street of Flers followed by our cheering infantry in pursuit of the retreating enemy.' Well it didn't seem quite like that to me from near Longueval on the west side of Delville Wood but that was a little over two kilometres from Flers. It was the only time I saw tanks in France.

*   *   *

I need not have worried about a haircut before going into the Somme battle. We marched through Albert to camp on a wide open down called The Sand Pits. Heavy gunfire to the north-east warned us what we must face, but first the whole battalion was ordered a haircut – everyone from the Colonel to the latest reinforcements from Blighty. A few packing cases served as barbers' chairs. We queued for turns and the barbers did the job at high speed. No question of 'Which side for a parting?' or 'How short d'you like it on top, sir?' The only parting was parting with all our hair, and short was as close to the scalp as clippers could cut. Such wholesale reaping enforced on all alike was accepted without protest, indeed occasioned much laughter and wit.

'What's the big idea, Bert?'

'An issue of feather beds, chum. 'Stead of kipping on this bloody 'ard ground: but the QM Stores is short of feathers for our beds so we're 'aving human 'air instead.'

'You got it wrong, Alf. It's to surprise Jerry. When he sees an army of bald 'eads he'll think we're supermen from Mars.'

But the real joke, causing frequent and continuous laughter, was eight hundred shorn officers, NCOs and men all looking alike. No one recognised anyone: I was ages finding brother officers (strange to say, when I did spot them I couldn't recall their names). I walked right past the CO without knowing him. And when at last we were more or less sorted out I couldn't believe several in my platoon were my men at all. Then to my surprise I saw one man with quite a mop of hair, all the longer because the only one in the battalion. He was the MO.

'Hello, doctor,' I exclaimed, 'how did you escape?'

'The Sand Pits is as near as I go to any fighting,' he said, 'so I can keep my wool.'

'What's the big idea? What does it mean for us?'

'Head wounds galore.'

Next day we were given a refresher course on bayonet fighting. Someone in authority had been told that in trenches hand-to-hand fighting is rare, bayonets used in various ways but not as intended. None of that 'in . . . out . . . on to the next'. The course was supervised by army instructors, themselves too old for personal experience of practical war. I wondered what my mentor Hardy would think of it – probably an outburst on last-war-mentality. Perhaps in this Somme battle it would be different.

When war began everyone in England turned from the bickering of politicians to venerate one man, a military hero, Kitchener – 'K of K.' He'd almost saved Gordon from murder at Khartoum and finished off the long struggle against the Boers with victory for England.

Opinion in the front line about public leaders was remarkably uniform if a bit sweeping – Asquith didn't count, a nonentity; Lloyd George was despised, a mere politician; Winston Churchill was distrusted, always dashing around looking for the limelight; but the civilian sentiment for Kitchener was accepted in the army without qualification. When K of K was drowned, we looked at one another blankly – who then could lead England to victory? The rumour that the famous soldier had visited the trenches, and afterwards declared our war to be unlike any warfare he'd experienced, a war he didn't understand, bore the stamp of reality. How could this trench barrier be broken to bring about the kind of traditional war Kitchener did understand? We talked about an inevitable Big Push – cynically adding, 'ours or theirs?' We joked about it. *The New Church Times* had a comic advertisement – 'William O.N. Zollern at The New Church Hippodrome in his screamingly funny farce, *The Big Push* or *Over-Dun*.'

The Battle of the Somme began twenty-five days after

Kitchener was drowned. The first official news of the battle declared, 'We have pushed the enemy back, taken the initiative, captured many prisoners.' What we did not know, what no one in England knew (except presumably the War Office and the War Cabinet), was that there had been no breakthrough, only short advances measured in yards, enemy losses heavy, ours appalling. Nothing decisive: attacks and counter-attacks day after day, week after week, little patches of ground gained and lost again, regiments in action for a short time in one part of the battle, then moved to another part, then withdrawn. From when my battalion arrived at the Sand Pits near Albert to when we were withdrawn and began our long march back to Ypres, was exactly thirty-eight days.

The battle petered out in November. English and French historians say that the Somme battle was almost useless from a military point of view, but history meant nothing to us, we knew only our day-to-day experiences.

The mass hair-cropping at The Sand Pits camp, with the MO's cryptic comment on head wounds, should have set us wondering. What first struck me was the very different kind of country about us – instead of the flat Flanders plain, with straight tree-lined roads and unhedged farmland, the river Somme and its tributaries ran through gentle valleys in undulating country, with low hills rising to ridges or plateaux, set about with numerous small woods and fields with hedges.

Infantry live in the open, with makeshift shelters, so the nature of the soil is important. The Somme country is chalk to a great depth. The first trenches I saw, just captured from the enemy, were dry, strong in construction, with steps going down about fifteen feet underground into large dug-outs giving complete protection from gunfire, even the sound of shells bursting at ground level was masked. Superficial differences – but obviously the routine of trench life in the Salient did not apply here. The enemy fell back on prepared positions in a well-planned second line of defence.

For several days my battalion occupied a captured village awaiting orders. Waiting . . . waiting . . . waiting, as though having been brought to the verge of the Big Push no one knew what to do with us. My recollections of these to-and-fro movements is confused, because I couldn't see any connection between one event and another. It wasn't thought necessary to enlighten junior officers. I record brief accounts of my experiences during our thirty-eight days in what was probably the most costly battle in British history, they are set down in more or less chronological order based on notes written at the time on the back of maps or in my diary, illustrating the confusion of war – the mixture of personal and general, sport and light-heartedness with tragedy, horror and humour.

A few German dead still lying about rotting in this summer heat. No one's job to bury them I suppose, or no time: rather horrible to contemplate, attitudes often unnatural, especially when limbs gone, or entrails torn away.

Church Parade in an orchard, trees uprooted or shattered by shell fire, sound of distant guns where battle is raging along enemy second line of defence. Wonder how many will be at next church parade?

My younger sister's birthday. Casualties from shelling. Two subalterns killed. Slept in one of Jerry's deep dug-outs, about twenty feet underground, curious feeling that any ghosts will be hostile.

4.30 a.m. moved to Trones Wood. Thankful to be going anywhere from the trench we'd been in because impossible to bury dead horse – stank horribly, worse than dead men smell. Ordered to attack enemy at Guillemont, came under heavy machine gun fire before we got anywhere near objective. Dodged from shell hole to shell hole, but couldn't even see enemy machine gun emplacements. Had to abandon attack. Considerable casualties.

Night of torrential rain. Soaked to the skin. Whatever happens, men never miss chance to turn to sport. Hardly back from abortive attack on Guillemont, than patch of very wet ground was named The Oval, and inter-company cricket matches began. D Company beat A.

Took ration party carrying water in petrol cans to Hampshires cut off yesterday near Arrow Head Copse. Set out at 4 a.m., crawled much of the way to avoid machine gun fire. Back at 11 a.m. exhausted, wet from sudden heavy rain, but no casualties. In afternoon battalion ordered to renew attack on Guillemont. Rumours said RA had difficulty moving up heavy guns. Only field-gun support available for us, too light to silence enemy machine guns. Took cover when possible in shell holes, casualties heavy. Stretcher-bearers unable to evacuate wounded, some died in silence, others screaming in agony. After advance of only few yards, had to lie low till dusk, then creep back. I lost a sergeant, two lance-corporals, and eight men killed, as well as wounded.

Withdrawn to Transport Lines in Happy Valley. Everyone rather depressed. Played cricket for Officers v Transport.

Very hot again. Bathed in Ancre, very dirty stream crowded with army bathers. Cricket – D beat B.

Brigade Inspection. Goodness knows why. Perhaps to see if we need still more reinforcements. In last few days two subalterns killed, one missing, five wounded.

Slight attack of dysentery, sent for three days to camp near Bray-sur-Somme, inhabited village ten kilometres from fighting area. Shared tent with temporary Captain in Middlesex Regt. In tent opposite ours HRH The Prince of Wales on a Cook's Tour of the Front. He's not allowed near any fighting of course, chap on his staff says he's unconventional, impatient of old fogeys, wants to be up-to-date, forward-looking. We watched his coming and going, talking and laughing with his staff. Sometimes he nodded our way affably. We concluded he's indignant at this Cook's Tour, a sham pretence to make people at home believe he's doing his bit with us.

Another ration-party job. Ten men each with 2 gallon can of water and sandbag of food, searching for East Sussex cut off two days ago; thought to be holding out, no one knew exactly where. No established front line, so moved forward cautiously from Delville Wood towards Ginchy, unlimited No-Man's-Land. Here and there small groups of men from various regiments, uncertain where the enemy was, no news of any East Sussex. Hard work for my men with heavy loads, so left them under cover in a sunken road, went forward alone, reconnoitering. Shell-hole to shell-hole crawling confused my sense of direction. Soon hopelessly lost, didn't know if I was facing enemy or our starting point from the wood. Came upon wounded Yorkshire Light Infantryman in shell hole, gave him drink from my water-bottle. Said I'd return with more – a promise I knew would be difficult to keep. Saw a shelter scooped in a bank some way ahead with a man lying full length, back to me. Called as loudly as I dared, evidently asleep, possibly wounded. Took several minutes crawling to him. He didn't answer, so pulled his shoulder – dead, his face a terrible sight, eyes, nose and mouth buzzing with flies. A little further on saw a Jerry patrol. About turn, took ages to find sunken road where I'd left my men. Artillery fire increased, so decided to abandon task. When rejoined battalion Adjutant seemed disappointed, as though he thought I might have done better. Had to assure myself I had done all possible, but a sense of this failure hung about in my thoughts.

The most dreadful picture in my Somme gallery is a landscape – a wide upland slope, uniformly drab, dirty white, chalk mixed with decaying vegetation, not a tree stump or bush left, just desolation, with a track named Crucifix Alley for men to walk round or through shell holes to the larger desolation of Delville Wood. The whole blasted slope dotted to the very edges with dead bodies, too many to bury, and too costly, the area being under constant fire from artillery. This awful display of dead men looked like a set piece, as though some celestial undertaker had spaced the corpses evenly for interment and then been interrupted. Several times I picked a way through this cemetery of the unburied. A landscape picture my memory turns up in horror.

In the very middle of the Battle of the Somme, during a short lull when we were being re-formed and reinforced after heavy casualties, I was ordered to spend one day outside the combat area as Prosecutor on Courts-Martial, trying cases of desertion. Considerable publicity was given to such cases as a deterrent. Men found guilty were shot. I do not know if the civilian population in England knew about them, but in 1983 the War

Office records of cases in 1914–1918 were made available to historians.

Why was I picked for this rather grim task? Someone said, 'Golly! You landed a cushy job!' but that was facetious, with a touch of envy perhaps. We guessed a high authority, in the Way-Back behind the real war, ordered our battalion to provide one subaltern for one day and chance picked on me. None of us knew anyone who'd had such an experience, none of us knew anything at all of the procedures of Courts-Martial, or what a Prosecutor did.

In the course of the day I discovered that Military Law is different to Civil Law. I served on three courts, the members – a President, usually a Colonel, and two other senior officers. They came from different units, and did not try accused from their own regiments. As Prosecutor I was not a member of the Court, had no vote in the decisions or sentences. My job was to read aloud to the Court all the evidence they must consider, favourable or unfavourable to the accused. The evidence of desertion was always irrefutable, the accused being caught in the act – he should have been with his unit, and had been found somewhere else. The verdict was certain, the punishment already determined – shot by a firing squad of his own unit (i.e. by his comrades). It seemed to me the Court proceedings were mere formality. No doubt the same can be said often of Civil Law; but here in war, in front line war, formality was fatuous.

When I got back to the battalion my friends asked questions – on Court procedure, how long did each case take, did the guilty hear the sentence calmly, did I feel any personal responsibility? 'Obeying orders which we can't dodge absolves us of all responsibility,' I observed; and went on to add that the execution of a few miserable deserters seemed to me unimportant when the day before yesterday eight chaps in my platoon were killed and as like as not there would be as many or more tomorrow. Several of my companions nodded agreement. One, a law student who came to us from The Inns of Court OTC said, 'Damned lucky for you to get that experience.'

A month later I had the same job of Prosecutor again. The Adjutant picked on me, no doubt remembering I'd done it before. And seven months later I did it yet a third time, but with rather different feelings. As a general observation I'd say we PBI at the Front had no contempt for Deserters such as we felt for Scrimshankers and Base-Wallahs. Deserters had volunteered to serve King and Country, but when they came out found war was unlike what they supposed and they just couldn't take it (as had been so nearly my reaction to the Little Willie shell). Others may have overcome fear at first with courage but their courage had worn thin, as courage always does in time: they'd gradually cracked up, and tried to get away without plan or hope. They deserved pity, not contempt.

A fine autumn day, cloudless sky, a soft breeze. Good weather for our march. At last, we had been withdrawn from the Somme battle to march to a railhead on the way back to Ypres. We left Happy Valley at 8.30 a.m., and were now, in mid-morning, clear of Albert, beyond the range of artillery. The Virgin of Albert church still clung to her Child. So much for the end of war! In fields beside the road farmers were getting in their crops, 'fed and watered by God's Almighty hand' as the German harvest hymn puts it. I'm sure I had a humble thankful heart, and I dare say every man in the battalion felt the same.

Before we came to the Somme, while still in the familiar trenches of the Ypres Salient, the battalion's strength was made up to about eight hundred men, perhaps a few more. I never saw any official statistics of casualties on the Somme but some days it seemed as though almost the whole battalion had been wiped out: reinforcements turned up, usually in odd numbers from other units, a kind of patching of our torn garments with odd bits from a rag bag. Then would come another order – over the top again, another go at yesterday's objective, another decimation. As usual we PBI didn't kill; we were victims of artillery fire and especially of machine gun fire. A gunner told me his six-inch howitzers were stuck in shell holes where the front line had been, they couldn't be moved forward to shell the Bosche second line defence positions. He said the enemy had five times as many guns per kilometre of front line as we had. But in my experience our losses were mostly from machine guns, well sited to give overlapping fire and so cleverly concealed that we rarely saw them.

Now as we marched away from the Somme in drill-book fashion, the Colonel and the Adjutant riding at the head of the column, junior officers on foot with their platoons, we were a remnant. Was the Somme an old-fashioned kind of battle, left over so to say from the kind of war which Kitchener understood? Perhaps we were too closely involved to judge, couldn't see the wood for the trees. Wood for the trees! How cliché sayings trip us up! This thought is brushed off instantly by its literal irony – there *were* no trees, not anywhere, not in Delville Wood, or Trones Wood, or Bernafay Wood, or High Wood, or the smaller woods on the outskirts of villages at Ginchy and Guillemont and Montauban. Gone, all gone. I'd been in all those woods, and seen only tree stumps a few feet high, so quickly man destroys what nature has done in patient years. Nature herself would not recognise her creation in the devastated countryside of the Somme. God knows it had a bumper harvest too – acres and acres of dead and rotting bodies, ours and theirs, and no one with time and opportunity to bury them: as though Death had been walking to and fro in agitation, so much to do, so little time for any refinements of slaughter. Well, thank God, we were marching away from it, already several kilometres west of Albert.

My reflections were interrupted. The Adjutant rode back telling the men as he passed, 'Keep well over to your left, make room for a cavalcade to pass.' He spoke excitedly, and when he reached me said, 'General Haig is riding this way with his staff, alongside us in a minute or two. Order your men to march to attention, ready to salute.' Sir Douglas Haig! A chance encounter? Surely not. Planned so he could praise us for what the battalion had done. But when he was close I saw a man, stern faced, expressing no emotion, riding slowly, his thoughts elsewhere, for he left it to one of his Staff Officers to acknowledge the salutes of our platoons as he passed. We were none of us spit-and-polish soldiers like those admired in Blighty at military tournaments, pageants, or marching with well-trained precision on Horse Guards Parade. We were an exhausted remnant, torn uniforms, rifles slung over shoulders anyhow, boots uncleaned for weeks, puttees slack, but all remarkably content to be alive.

'Thirteen Platoon . . . eyes right.' I made my personal salute as smart as I could. But it was a poor show really, too thin, not enough of us – in my platoon only me and four men. All the same I felt I was acting in a bit of drama. I had saluted the C in C. As he rode on towards the distant rumble of battle I completed our salute, 'Thirteen Platoon . . . eyes front . . . march at ease.' I had saluted Sir Douglas Haig, Commander-in-Chief of the British Army, and was proud to have done so as I think my four men were proud. Something to tell them at home one day.

I had been in the Somme battle and I saw it – but only with the eyes of a junior officer. I didn't believe the official reports that all was going well – 'enemy pushed back . . . no longer able to stem our advance . . . German counter-attacks too late to be effective' and so on. But General Haig planned its strategy and tactics, declared that every step in his plan had been taken with Divine help. For me the honour of saluting the C in C was the finale of a large experience. Ypres was rightly known as 'the bloody salient'. There we were familiar with Death (which might interrupt a joke, or the reading of a home letter, or a game of *vingt-et-un*) and our casualties were constant and heavy, but the Somme revealed Life at its last gasp.

CHAPTER SEVEN

The Russian Sap:
First Leave

I remember I had a War Office map 'with trenches corrected to October 1915', some 'disused or doubtful', and a footnote which made me laugh aloud: 'obstacles such as wire entanglements, thickset hedges, are often omitted in front line trenches in order to keep the map clear.' So encouraging to have a nice clear map; much nicer than knowing what one might have to face.

A trench my men held, once we were back near Ypres, crossed what had been a main road from Messines to Armentières. At that junction of road and trench, a sap (surprisingly called Russian Sap) had been pushed forward into No-Man's-Land, ending as a listening post. This sap dived from the front trench under the disused road, through a tunnel coming up on the other side of the road in No-Man's-Land with a slightly enlarged open end where at night, but not during the day, two men kept watch ('kept listening' would be more precise), to get early warning of any enemy approach.

An incident occurred at Russian Sap of no general importance, but significant for me. I was on duty one morning when I heard a 5.9 shell land near the sap. Hurrying there, I found a group of my men in some confusion.

'Men in there, sir . . . buried,' cried one, pointing to the sap entrance.

'How many?'

'Don't exactly know, sir,' said a man with a bloody hand from a wound. He named three, and concluded, 'more than them went in'. I'd often seen men afeared, with wind up, but I guessed these men were unusually flustered because guilty, knowing an order had been disobeyed. When I first saw Russian Sap I realised that men in the front trench would be tempted to use it as a shelter from ill-weather or shell fire, and it could be a trap, the tunnel under the road not deep enough to withstand a direct hit. So I had given an order that the sap must never be used as a shelter, but only for going to or from the listening post at night.

The sap entrance had caved in. I ran to it and began throwing out rubble – stones, small rocks, quite big dry lumps of earth. I soon saw there was no chance to clear it. In a fury I returned to the trench. 'Damned fools,' I cried, 'you all know my orders. Couldn't one of you have stopped those who went in? They're probably dead now; anyway we can't get to them.' I heard a movement behind me and turning, saw the Battalion Intelligence Officer, chap named Watson, standing listening to my diatribe. Watson slept and fed at Battalion HQ, but his job often brought him to the front trench. We were good friends, and I was just a little disconcerted that he had heard me talking angrily to my men. 'Don't let me interrupt you,' he said mildly without a shadow of sarcasm. Then, seeing I was nonplussed, nodded to me in a friendly way, and observed reflectively, 'the listening-post end of the sap may not be blocked.'

'Men inside probably dead, but we can't get to them till after dark anyhow.'

'One or two may be alive but trapped . . . might be worth making a dash over the top to the listening post now . . . find out the position at that end.'

I stared at Watson in astonishment – over the top in daylight, a crazy idea! I'd never forgotten Sergeant Hill's warning to me, *not even a quick look over the parapet or Top-notcher might get you.* This had been confirmed for me weeks later when a newcomer from Blighty was being shown round the front trench: he had been given the usual warning, but hadn't taken it seriously – he collapsed against me, his brains (and a bit more) blown out by a sniper. And now my good friend Watson suggested a much bigger risk, crawling or scrambling or upright running, twenty-five to thirty yards to the listening-post – in daylight.

'Job for Intelligence,' he observed.

'Not you,' I said firmly. 'If anyone goes it's me . . . my trench . . . my men.'

'Your trench, your duty to be here,' he replied, and then laughed, made a joke of it. 'I'm not a company officer like you, I'm only Intelligence, Old Man, Intelligence is always expendable.'

We both accepted the common judgement – to be seen by the enemy was asking to be shot. I wasn't personally afraid to take the risk, my view was academic. For a moment we argued. Then Watson took off his trench coat and moved towards the firing step. At once I did the same. I couldn't let him go . . . if it was anyone's job it was mine. I saw his determination and hastened to be before him. Perhaps one of us was justified in taking such a gamble but certainly not both of us. I was on the firing step a few seconds before him and about to scramble over the parapet when I realised that the first to show himself, over the top crossing No-Man's-Land, would have a slightly better chance than the one who came after: before a sniper fired he would see the second figure and choose him as the better target, giving a longer time to aim. So I held back till Watson was clear of our trench and running in No-Man's-Land. Then I followed.

I'm sure we were both surprised to find ourselves lying in the listening post without a shot having been fired. The sap tunnel wasn't blocked at that end, so I crawled in at once, followed closely by Watson. Soon my torch revealed a considerable block where the roof had collapsed. The silence was intense, as though we were at the bottom of a deep well. In the dim light I could just make out the back of a man, head touching the ground, body wedged between sandbags and rubble. Any attempt to move that body would surely bring down what little remained of the tunnel where we crouched. Chap must be dead, I told myself – and I had a lot of experience.

'A Goner,' I reported to Watson, and spoke the hard word softly as though we were taking part in a religious ceremony in a church where convention demanded a pious hush.

'Sure he's dead?' asked Watson. 'You near enough to feel his heart or a pulse?'

'Nothing we can do.'

Nothing? My own words disclosed to me in a flash of understanding that I had developed an obsession, an irrational concept which must have grown, week by week, month by month, till now it was a *fait accompli*. When first I came to the Front that Little Willie shell put me in a panic because of its inhuman power, now I was often afraid when I heard death coming my way but it wasn't an obsession. I sometimes took a hand in burying corpses, or reburying them after they were disinterred by shells. I knew that dead men and bits of bodies are the trademarks of war. Only the sentimentalists, blinded by Glory-War, think of war without dead bodies. I reminded myself that a dead man is dead, his life ended (or gone elsewhere), his body empty; but in Russian Sap I found I could not press close to that body, though I believed him to be a Goner. I could not feel about under the shirt for a heartbeat. I was the victim of an obsession.

'He's dead all right,' I asserted, without answering Watson's explicit question.

'Damned difficult to feel a heartbeat when it's weak,' Watson said, 'Let me try.' He pushed past me and I watched with some shame as he put an arm over the man's body, pushed and pulled seeking a pulse in the body I could not touch. Watson's examination confirmed the chap was dead, the body empty. But I had failed to make sure as I ought to have done: that was the dreadful obsession I now must admit to myself. I feared my friend would have sensed my weakness. As we crawled back to the open listening post he said sympathetically, 'Intelligence makes one over-curious, wasting effort turning over stones and exploring avenues, as the politicians say. My job as IO is cushy compared with yours, Old Man.'

When we were about to make the dash back to the safety of the front trench Watson observed, 'We were damned lucky on our run out. Snipers must be having a late breakfast, stuffing German sausages probably.' I, too, had been thinking of the return. Snipers, I thought, must be exceptionally cruel men watching and watching for the pleasure of killing; even if they are not on the look-out now, the Bosche sentries will have noticed some unusual movements, and have a machine gun trained on our listening post. When they see two of us on the run they will fire at the second.

'Same order going back,' I said. 'You first.' I was choosing the bigger risk in an effort to restore my morale. Watson went. I followed, expecting every second to hear the stutter of a machine gun or more likely feel a knock-out blow.

A Captain (commanding C Company) was in our trench when we tumbled down into safety.

'God Almighty!' he exclaimed. 'You been over the top . . . both of you . . . in broad daylight!'

This incident was talked about in the regiment, became a legend, even a subject of gossip in other battalions of our brigade; some spoke of it as almost incredible, certainly brave: but I knew the truth. I had been overwhelmed by an obsession, surrendered to fear, a foolish fear of touching a harmless dead man, an empty body. And I was ashamed.

When I was a young child Life and Death presented themselves not as any sort of problem, but as simple concepts – I was alive, so was my brother, and my parents, and a pet cat, and a dog, and mice in the kitchen, birds in the garden, rabbits on the Common, and lots of other creatures. Some vanished mysteriously like the cat's kittens, some died sooner or later, and so it would be for my brother and me. All children acquire some such easy knowledge of Life and Death without thinking, but gradually, an adult finds Death to be a mystery hanging around his mind asking to be explained. Religious teaching sometimes offers adequate explanation but more often the explanation comes with self-knowledge gained in the course of living. Perhaps my obsession, which came to light in Russian Sap, helped me to an early appreciation that Life and Death are a unity; opposites but complementary.

By 1916 all the combatants had many more guns than they had when war began and as the war continued the volume of artillery fire increased considerably. It was not merely the volume of weaponary but the variety too. Quite the most important was our Tank. Four months after I saw the first few on the Somme, infantry officers were invited to apply for transfer from the PBI to a Tank Corps being formed as a new branch of the army. Every subaltern in our battalion applied. It was obviously not a 'cushy' job, no joke shut up in a large tinbox under enemy gunfire, wouldn't appeal to scrimshankers; but an honourable escape from the front line. We were agog at the prospect, couldn't stop discussing the pros and cons – all pros it seemed to us: no longer PBI, almost certainly some training in Blighty . . . only occasional short periods in action . . . the rest of life well out of the fighting area . . . probably in

comfortable civilian billets . . . with French rations . . . sleep all
night in real beds . . . no rats, no lice. Of course we all applied.
A Tank Corps Selection Board was housed at Philosophe and I
found myself back in the derelict village I knew. At the interview mention was made of my comparatively long experience
in trenches. I came away full of hope but although six of our
battalion were accepted, and transferred then and there, I was
not one. The six all had knowledge of mechanical engineering,
driving a car or some appropriate hobby. Disappointing, but it
seemed reasonable. A week later three of the lucky six were sent
back to the battalion because too many had been accepted!

After the Tank I think the most effective new weapon was the
German *Minenwerfer*, known to all our chaps as a 'minnie'. It
was a trench gun with a range of about five hundred yards. It
threw a mine packed with explosive straight up into the air
from one side of No-Man's-Land to fall on or about our trench
opposite. The effect was devastating. A direct hit of one 'minnie' could blow to smithereens eight to ten yards of well-
constructed trench. When a *minenwerfer* was fired we could hear
distinctly a mild 'poof' from the Bosche trench; at once we
scanned the sky above with absolute concentration because the
'minnie' became visible for two seconds only as it reached the
top of its trajectory and turned, hovering, before starting its
swift descent. This glimpse was just long enough to show where
the monster was likely to land, time to run a few feet right or left
before throwing oneself flat on the ground to minimise the
blast. I found 'minnies' put the wind up me more than anything
else, wondering if I'd really spotted the brute hovering in the
sky and then waiting for the thud when it landed.

It's all right to cry 'Welcome, wild North Easter' when you live
in a Berkshire rectory with a good coal fire like Charles
Kingsley, but living in trenches in the Ypres Salient through a

continental winter is a different matter. I've never known such cold as the winter of 1916–17. On Christmas Eve it snowed all day. Our world was an ocean of snow, not deep but spread everywhere – no life but ours, no smoke rising from any human habitation, no boats moving on frozen canals, everything locked in an Ice Age. For six weeks the walls of our shallow dug-outs were papered over with thin ice, frozen water from the permanently wet soil. We had a small coke-burning brazier (fuel supply uncertain) and sometimes managed to get up a fug. The men were generally less fortunate; many went down with what was called 'trench fever', some with severe frostbite.

Someone at home sent me a pocket medicine wallet intended for explorers, with small sheets of gelatine impregnated with common medicines – quinine, aspirin, cascara and concentrated ginger. I found this ginger effective when I was through-and-through cold. Apart from feeling the cold I wasn't troubled by exposure, indeed I was quite fit. One night we were relieved and went back for Rest to the coalmining village of Philosophe, which had been knocked about earlier in the war. While I settled my men in a forsaken monastery my batman found a place for me in a house with an undamaged roof but a large hole in the side wall from a direct hit by a shell. In an upstairs room someone had fixed rabbit wire over the frame of a bedstead. With a mattress of empty sandbags and a couple of army blankets, this was luxury, though the large hole in the outside wall let in a lot of night air. I hadn't undressed for a week so it was good to take off my outer clothes and get under the blankets. A whole night of undisturbed sleep! I told my batman, 'Call me in the morning when the cookhouse has made tea', and I dare say I was asleep before he got down the rickety stairs. It was dark when I awoke, frozen cold, the blankets on the floor. I tried to retrieve them but couldn't move, not a muscle, couldn't sit up. It must have been hours later when my batman brought me tea and found me unconscious. I suppose stretcher-bearers carried me to an ambulance but I really didn't know anything till I began to feel warm in a bed in an Advanced Casualty Hospital. The doctor diagnosed 'Myalgia' (a grand name for muscular rheumatism), temperature 103. After a few days in bed – glorious days of sleep and warmth – he said, 'Not a Blighty case, I'm afraid, you'll be A1 in three or four weeks. I'm sending you to a Base Hospital . . . make the most of it . . . a real holiday from trenches.'

I knew that when the Base Hospital discharged me I might be sent to any unit which happened to be under strength. I explained to the MO that I'd been a long time with my regiment, and should hate to be sent to any other. He was sympathetic, said he would send me to an Officers' Convalescent Home at Aire-sur-la-Lys, an inhabited town in the Pas de Calais, but they didn't keep anyone longer than two weeks, then I should have to return to my regiment.

Aire was a welcome liberty from the isolation of trench life. By the second week I went short distances on crutches, exploring the old town. On my last day I discovered a small bookshop which had a shelf of English books. To my delight I saw Palgrave's *Golden Treasury*, an anthology of poetry we'd used at school. My father was a great reader, used to read poems aloud to us children. I bought this book and still have it, my name written on the title page, with 'Aire-sur-la-Lys' and the date XI.III.XVII. For the rest of my time in France I carried this precious volume always in my pack. In one dug-out I hung the pack on a nail beside the shelf on which I slept. A few days later I put my hand in to get the book, rummaged about among spare socks, official documents, a sponge and razor and letters from home, and felt something soft moving, several things – baby rats! My loathing of rats was so strong I destroyed this addition to their population.

Glancing through my *Golden Treasury* I am interested to see the numerous underlinings I made – some sentimental, like Rossetti's 'Remember me when I am gone away, gone far away into the silent land', and Browning's 'Fear death – to feel the fog in my throat'. Others reveal that the excitement and intense concentration of my duties did not entirely prevent a young man's Spring fancy turning lightly to thoughts of love. Indeed, at the end of Palgrave's selection I wrote after the last poem words I chanced to come across – a woman to her husband, 'Tell me you love me so that when I dream I may dream of Love and when I sleep dreamless Love may be holding me in his wings . . . and when I die Love may be the Angel that takes me home.'

That was the only time I suffered from severe exposure in my trench life. The short holiday at Aire cured my muscles of Myalgia but did much more – it refreshed my mind with poetry and sentimentality.

No one has a right to Leave, it's a privilege – so the War Office reminded us. 'As if we don't *earn* a few days at home after six months in Hell,' someone grumbled. We all agreed. After I had been out twenty-three weeks, a clerk at Battalion HQ whispered to me, 'Saw your name on a Leave List, sir . . . any day now.' We were in a quiet sector near Vimy Ridge, so my hope ran high, ran so high it got out of breath and I began to fancy every shell coming anywhere near must have my name on it. Ten days later leave came officially, to start next morning after Dawn Stand-To. An anxious night! Enemy seemed more active than usual, but at last dawn came, as dawn does come, always reliable, early in summer, later in winter, whatever the weather. But man is capricious. With dawn came another order, 'Leave cancelled.' For three days my leave was subject to vacillation, 'leave tomorrow . . . leave postponed . . . leave at dawn . . . all leave cancelled.' One day at 4.30 a.m. (during an 'on' period), I bolted down a muddy communication trench (hidden from *notchers* by the ridge), towards Bethume, and thence to Boulogne. Next day I crossed to Folkestone, the U-boat menace temporarily under control.

Folkestone station on the South-Eastern and Chatham Railway was a model of civilisation, as though it spent every forenoon tidying itself to welcome returning heroes. The bookstall shouted familiar titles, *The Strand Magazine* (stories by P.G. Wodehouse, Phillips Oppenheim and Pett Ridge), *The Illustrated London News*, *The Wide World*, and serious weeklies like *The Spectator* and *Land and Water*, and, of course, *The Boys' Own Paper* and *Chums*. (Was it really only yesterday that I spent pocket money on these juvenile publications?) Being an officer I must travel first class, though my uniform was caked with dried Flanders mud. No difficulty in finding an empty compartment (the ambition of all English travellers). The few civilians on the platform were unmistakeably English, well-mannered, minding their own business, incurious of strangers, quietly dignified – such a contrast to voluble excited Frenchmen.

Kent, the garden of England. 'What should they know of England who only England know?' Such a contrast to the ugliness of trenches, with empty bully beef cans and man's indestructible litter, no wild flowers, plants or shrubs, nothing alive but us and rats.

Miles and miles of unspoiled Kent, bright in the evening sunlight, every small field a picture framed in a hawthorn hedge. Here and there majestic trees, silver birch, poplars (not the Lombardy ones), great elms and sycamore and horse chestnuts and lime and English oaks holding out wide-spreading branches of leaves ready to challenge the winds of autumn. Sometimes the train passed through a little wood (at the back of my mind those Somme woods with slivered tree trunks), sometimes a village with an old church, perhaps founded by Saxons or Normans, testifying to centuries of

107

security, untroubled by invading armies. Occasionally a manor house set in a formal garden peeping through a fringe of trees as though to see how Nature manages her freedom in the wide world. Peace everywhere, no ruins, no shell-holes disrupting the smooth green surface of meadows. A few men and women and children around farmsteads, a farmer striding along a path with his dog, a woman collecting washing from a clothes line, a pony trap raising a trail of white dust along a lane. I stared and stared, 'swallowing beauty' as the Chinese say. Other countries must have some beauty, even France (though not where I had been) but for me this journey through the garden of England, aroused a strong emotion – England a country to cherish, to protect, to fight for.

The Railway Company, attempting to restrain the increasing use of advertising hoardings, allowed one sign per mile, standing isolated in a field at a readable distance from the train, combining the advertisement with a notice of the distance from the terminus – London 30 miles, Beechams Pills Worth a Guinea a Box. London 29 miles, Zam Buck for a Healthy Skin. London 28 miles, Sunny Jim (jumping a fence) Force is the Food that Raises Him. So we approached the outer suburbs of the capital – large houses with big gardens, rich people sitting outside enjoying the evening sun, children at their last games before bed, a man mowing his lawn, a tennis court right alongside the railway, a mixed doubles with a girl serving (and I'd hardly seen a girl in six months, only slatternly wenches on French or Belgian farms).

The train whistled through stations, plunged into tunnels, clattered beside the high walls of cuttings; houses crowded together, gardens small, no tennis courts, no garden chairs, no suggestion of affluence or leisure. Then came factories and workshops making all manner of human wants – pottery, vinegar, drainpipes and guttering, jams, furniture, paint. A signal stopped my express on an embankment, overlooking on one side rows of narrow slum streets, mean buildings with tiny backyards, washing hanging on poles from upper windows, and scantily dressed children playing hop-scotch and tig; and on the other side of the embankment a large cemetery, consecrated ground, where civilians who died abed in old age could begin their long rest, decently packed in wooden boxes with brass handles, each coffin labelled to prevent mistakes at the Last Judgement. (How could I fail to think of young chaps I'd helped to bury uncoffined in Flanders' mud?) And I, having swallowed beauty, found now a rather bitter taste in my mouth.

I only dozed on the Flying Scotsman, it was so crowded and my thoughts, fully wound up, wouldn't stop. Agreed, we fight for England, the beauty of Kent and the Downs, but can a man die for a country? Would any man give his life for the most beautiful country in the world if it were uninhabited? Of course not; it's people we die for – those who live in the garden of England, and the prosperous few in the outlying suburbs of London and a number who find comfort and security in the lesser suburbs; but also for a multitude who struggle hand-to-mouth in crowded slums. Platitudes today; not so obvious in the class-conscious England of 1916.

At home everything was unchanged, going on as usual, as it seemed to me. The day started with family prayers before breakfast (as in many middle-class homes), my father reading a passage of scripture; my sisters turn and turn about saying grace before meals, 'for what we are about to receive . . .' I recalled occasions when my father reminded us children, 'It's not only food for which we are truly thankful, we receive everything from God, life itself.' So the habit went on, always had gone on, unquestioned by me until now. For my family, 'about to receive' implied no change – always the same, adequate food, same common round and trivial tasks. How could they understand the ever-changing quality of the Life I'd been clinging on to for the last six months? Did my father expect me to be truly thankful in advance for the hazards of trench life?

No matter! I found some satisfaction even in the unchanging pattern of home life; and not only at home. The neighbours I knew hadn't changed, still went about their customary affairs, men leaving home for offices, factories, university, teaching jobs – same time, almost to a minute every morning; housewives to and fro shopping, gardeners gardening, men with golf clubs, church-goers in their Sabbath best.

I noticed newcomers in the house opposite, in particular a girl dressed in black who came out every morning and walked smartly along the road to the tram stop in the main Liberton road. 'Who's the girl in black?' I asked my elder sister. To my surprise she knew the army song, *Mademoiselle from Armentières, parlez-vous?* from the early days of the war. She at once teased me with this song, saying the newcomer probably came from Armentières. My young sister joined in this teasing, made up a song which began 'Alack, Alack, the girl in black'. I told them not to be cheeky, but in fact I rather enjoyed a little romantic speculation. One morning I actually followed this girl to the tram stop and stood beside her waiting for the tram. That's as far as I got, but I did better with a girl my sister brought home from school. It was a 'done thing' for young officers to ask girl friends to meet them mid-morning at the west end of Princes Street and have tea or coffee or cocoa with shortbread at Mackies. I persuaded one of my sister's friends to meet me on my only Saturday morning, her day off from school.

There are no heroes in trenches, reality is too close to the PBI for Glory-War. But on leave I was a hero, everyone I knew and sometimes strangers told me I was a hero: they were not interested to hear talk about trench life, how we lived, what we did by day and all night. It was as though calling us heroes was enough, they didn't know any higher praise, and so they felt absolved from any effort to understand the nature of war. For my part it was sufficient that I had overcome my first cowardice, the Little Willie shell, and was now able to avoid showing when I had the wind up. I was patriotic, England came first (not Great Britain, because at that time the wide world spoke of England including Scotland, Wales and Ireland) and I didn't think it unchristian to pray, 'confound their politics, frustrate their knavish tricks'. I didn't want to recount horrors to my parents of course, nor to young girls like my sisters; indeed I wanted to forget horrors while on leave, and forget too the whole background of devastation. I explained a few comic happenings, like the General and my earrings. When I told that story at dinner my sisters thought it very funny; my mother said angrily, 'old fool ought to be reduced to the ranks', and my father went silent, his lips compressed.

My mother sometimes asked questions about my personal comfort – more socks needed? Food parcels arrive intact? – and once my father took me aside – 'Your brother's grave – have you ever heard of the place Vlamertinghe?' I didn't know how to tell him that I had been there but not looked upon the grave. He wouldn't understand, how could he with his conventional ideas of Christian burial and all the saints resting from earthly labours? I said, 'I know where the place is, Dad. It's a village near Ypres. Some day when we're near I'll manage to get to it and let you know.'

Eight days leave – and eight peaceful nights at home. Reunion with family and friends, beauty of the English countryside (no longer taken for granted but contrasted with the desolation of trenches) and enjoyment of the real luxuries of civilisation – a bed at night, undisturbed sleep, clean clothes, hot water and a bath: inevitably these delights ended in a

111

railway station farewell. Waverley Station, with its customary bustle, was silent to us – solemn as a funeral, and without the customary clock-watching remarks of farewells – 'so nice to see you . . . come again soon . . . can always put you up . . . don't leave it so long next time.' Nothing for us to talk about, absolutely nothing. My parents did what they could to look cheerful, but my mother faltered as she asked, 'When is your next leave due?' On the tip of my tongue to chant the children's 'this year, next year, sometime, never', but I realised that would be too lighthearted, too evasive, too frightening, I replied, 'Leave is always uncertain in the army, but the war can't go on much longer – starving Germans won't face another winter, reckon I'll be home by Christmas.' For the first time I gave a momentary thought to the strain the war must be for parents, but it was very much of a passing thought: even in the depressing sadness of farewell my mind was across the Channel, wondering if I'd find anyone I knew at the Officers' Club in Boulogne, and which trenches my men would be holding now, probably beyond Noeux-les-Mines. I wanted the magic word 'Christmas' to spell hope to my mother, but the end of my leave was sad.

I had an extra cause for unhappiness, too, a personal involvement in a tragic event. A family named MacGreen lived next door: the father a bank manager, two girls and a boy Jimmy, same age as me. Jimmy went to our school and became my closest friend, in and out of our house as though one of the family. We played golf together on the Braid Hills, and shared various hobbies. Like all our age group Jimmy was crazy to volunteer when war began. We had sat side-by-side at our school desks filling in our applications for commissions in the Special Reserve, but when he took his form home for his father to sign, Mr MacGreen refused. Jimmy wasn't far from tears when he told us.

'My pater says the war will last another three years, and when I'm discharged from the army I'd have no qualifications for any permanent employment.'

'Same for all of us.'

'He says I must get some training now, preferably in science.'

'Fat lot of good that'll be if we lose the war.'

'He says older men should fight, they can go back to work they know. He says I shall live another fifty years after the war, and I must qualify for a respectable occupation.'

'Rotten luck, old man,' was all we could say.

When I went to the Channel Islands I rather forgot Jimmy. He wrote several times, at first hopefully – so many casualties he thought his pater must change his mind. Then came a short letter. Mr MacGreen had apprenticed him to a small firm of analytical chemists. He had protested, had a great row, but was obliged by law to obey his father till he came of age at twenty-one.

I heard no more till I sent Jimmy a Field Service postcard from the Front giving my address. 'God how I envy you,' he replied, but he didn't complain about his work. The lab. was short of staff and he often worked alone analysing all sorts of substances, some for what he called forensic medicine. His letter ended, 'the present is the only time that matters, who wants a long safe life after the war? This lab. is my funk hole.'

As soon as I came on leave I asked my elder sister if she'd seen Jimmy lately. Her grimace indicated more than indifference, contempt. 'Haven't spoken to him since he became a chemist or something. He's not been to see us. Ashamed no doubt, as he jolly well ought to be.' I knew the laboratory, a small building opposite the Herriot-Watt Museum in Chambers Street. One day I went to see Jimmy. He was alone, making an analysis; he put down a bottle labelled *potassium cyanide*, and stared at me as though I were a total stranger. He looked quite old, face very white and expressionless as if his thoughts were set in plaster of paris. Waiting for a response to my cheerful greeting I reflected that working indoors all day and in the chemical stinks of a lab. might account for his unhealthy appearance. When he spoke his few bitter words astounded me. I should have guessed we had no common interests now. Clearly my unexpected visit disturbed him deeply. Perhaps he thought I came in pity. I left abruptly, feeling a little hurt by his apparent hostility.

Two days later my sister told me the MacGreen girls had not turned up at school, some talk of an accident to their brother. Next day everyone knew. Jimmy had been found dead on the floor of his lab. Mr MacGreen was distraught. 'An accident,' he declared, 'a terrible accident. No one knows how it happened.' The family doctor thought it must be poisoning, probably gas fumes produced while making an analysis. Mr MacGreen kept on repeating, 'an accident, no one knows how it happened' and told anyone who would listen that Jimmy had settled down so happily, liked his work, was doing well.

No one knew how it happened; but I did. In trenches we put together two ordinary words, joined by a hyphen to make a new word with rather a pathetic meaning – 'self-inflicted'.

CHAPTER EIGHT

Hans and Courts-Martial

When I came face to face with Hans he was dead. I knew nothing about the fellow, not his name of course, nor how long he'd been dead. To me he was a Jerry, just 'one of them'. I felt through his pockets, a routine procedure for Intelligence – carved Calabash pipe (very German, I thought contemptuously, myself smoking a Dunhill), a pouch covered in fur, penknife, copying-ink pencil, several much-folded letters, and a notebook. I'd like to have kept the pipe for my men (they'd have laughed at its swanky German appearance, tried smoking it turn and turn about), but both my side pockets carried Mills Bombs, so I'd only room for the letters and notebook, which might interest Intelligence. About a week later, when I'd forgotten about Hans, Watson brought me the notebook. 'Nothing in this for Intelligence,' he said, 'but it's amusing. Twenty-eight pages of dull diary in rather illiterate Bavarian–German, followed by English phrases the fellow thought would be useful if taken prisoner. *I demand to see Camp Commandant . . . I need food and drink . . . some place to sleep.* I reckon this fellow Hans would have given himself up if he'd seen half a chance. He was compiling a German-English glossary, and the last pages, in rather comical English, describe his going home on leave. You'll enjoy reading the funny bits: in fact you may like to keep the notebook as a souvenir.'

After the name HANS, written on the inside cover in the fancy script lettering Germans use for special names, newspaper and book titles, a space had been heavily blacked out, his

115

family name I suppose, a precaution in case the notebook was discovered by an officer. Hans, about the only German name I know, somehow sounds friendly, memories of *Grimm's Fairy Tales*, I suppose; the title of a story in my copy is 'Hans in Luck'.

'I resolve to write for exercises, some English language, and because What I wrote, will write, may not be read easily by other one else. How much my wish is that at school I am more serious with the English studies. But I shall make the amends.'

During the next few days I read and re-read all Hans had written in English. His home was on a farm in the state of Bavaria. He began with the joy of homecoming, 'I march in the lands of my ancestor farm. My parents do not learn that I am coming.' Hans approached the farmhouse by a stony cart track through a wood. First to greet him was his dog Rudolf who 'rushed from afar barking with delights'. Next his mother crying with 'the pleasures', tucking the 'soup broth cloth' into an apron pocket. His sisters, Lina and Sanna, caught sight of him in the farmyard as they came from work in the fields. Lina threw herself into his arms laughing. Sanna cried delightedly, 'Papa come and see who is here, it's Hans, the war is concluded.' That first evening Hans saw Jorinda. On every one of the seven days of leave, he had something to say about Jorinda. His father is shadowy, mentioned always with a fearful respect. I see the old farmer as a stern, stiff autocrat, grimly satisfied with duties – duty to the Kaiser, to Germany, to God; always duty and in that order. His mother makes Hans 'pies'. (In his glossary 'pies' is listed with a question mark, 'tarts or perhaps, confections?'). One evening Hans takes the three girls to the 'Kino'. 'We all make laughs at Charlie Chaplain who have much funny accidents, knocking over a market stall of fruits, upsetting a seat in the park which have a girl sitting on it.' Jorinda's brother, an engineer, tells them that soon moving pictures can be made to talk. Once Hans goes alone with

Jorinda to climb a hill to a 'Schloss'. She falls on a rock, breaking her 'Strumpfe' – a bone I suppose, but after the word 'breaks' Hans wrote 'perhaps cuts', so maybe 'Strumpfe' is not a bone. Hans describes Jorinda as 'a beautiness', and as his leave draws to a close he abandons caution – 'she is my heart love'. When the diary ends, with farewells at the 'Bahnhof', it is evident that Hans and Jorinda are very much in love.

How we betray ourselves by the things at which we laugh! I read aloud to the Mess parts of Hans' diary. The glossary made everyone laugh. Against the word 'daisies' he had written, 'some more meanings than the meadow flowers. Dictionary says "ball travelling along ground at cricket game," and English soldiers talk of "pushing up the daisies," perhaps when digging trenches?' 'Blighty' puzzled Hans. 'Dictionary says "blight is malignant influence," but English soldiers call their country Blighty.'

When we officers met together for meals there wasn't much to talk about, Hans' diary inspired light-hearted banter, and some imitation of foreigners trying to speak English (like 'Pidgin English' of army units serving in India and China). One wit made up a limeric using the words *Strumpfe* and *beautiness*.

I laughed with the others until someone made a surprising observation: 'Give the Hun his due. He was trying to teach himself English, a foreign language. None of us has any ambition to learn German, not even to swat up a few phrases.' But an old Captain who had just come to us from a Kitchener army unit said contemptuously, 'By all means give the Hun his due, serve him right, all Huns deserve to die, descendants of that butcher Genghis Khan.' This was a sentiment not general at this period of the war. Most PBI recognised that Germans were not all alike – Prussians were aggressive bullies, others from

Bavaria, Saxony, Württemburg, might be 'good' Germans.

When I was alone I read and re-read Hans' diary. His broken English made his descriptions vivid and drew out my imagination. I saw his home, a small but solid farmhouse, clean and well ordered, window-shutters painted green, curtains precisely matched, even the animals in the fields bright and glossy as in a child's Noah's Ark. I was a spectator of disciplined family life, children obedient to parents whom they respected, admired, loved: ordinary simply likeable people. I pictured the laughing Jorinda in a patterned cotton frock with a shiny belt, her straw-coloured hair in pigtails tied with blue ribbons – two pigtails like my elder sister at home when last I'd seen her. I saw these pictures with an inward eye's clarity, always in sunshine. And I wondered, how many days does it take the German War Office to inform the next-of-kin when a man is killed? Did the austere old farmer know yet? I could imagine him receiving the news, another duty to be accepted with stiff upper lip: and Jorinda . . . ?

I only saw Hans for a few moments, dead: but the notebook I took from his pocket carried within it a living seed which sprouted in my mind. In some mysterious way our lives seemed linked together. I felt I owed the fellow something, an obligation, rather as conscience may rebuke one mildly for the neglect of an old acquaintance or an unanswered letter or an invitation overlooked.

After the war I kept the notebook in my desk with other odds and ends of sentimental value – my Commission from King George V, a small trench mirror through which I'd often stared across No-Man's-Land, and trench maps, and my pocket diaries. Occasionally when turning over such trivia I re-read what Hans had written in English: no longer funny, mature now.

When the Hitler war seemed inevitable I wanted to return

the notebook to the family of Hans, to his sisters, or perhaps Jorinda, but I couldn't because I didn't know his surname or where they lived in the large State of Bavaria. So, for many years after my brief encounter with a dead enemy his notebook remained in my desk testifying to a complex emotion which I hardly understood.

About this time I made my last appearance in a Court-Martial. Something was different from the earlier occasions. I have a vivid recollection of the affair. My mind's eye can *see* the little hall in which the Court assembled, *see* the faces of the members, *see* myself too (back view, for I was facing the Court members), and I *hear* the rather socially-conscious accent of the President when he addressed me, and the deep bass of the Captain, and my own youthful voice with the slight Edinburgh accent picked up at school. Writing years later, the proceedings are before me as though they were a recent cinema film, featuring me as the star performer. I tell myself, that's exactly right, every detail, every spoken word. And then I stop to think about it and blurt out (in my mind) 'I know these things really happened beyond question, but could it have been *me*? Is it possible that memory plays me a trick? Was that Prosecutor some other fellow, not me?' I consult my diary and come to the relevant entry in March 1917: irrefutable evidence in my boyish writing set down that very day – confirming memory (see illustration).

Something was different. I was a veteran with eleven months' service, much of it in the Salient and on the Somme. I reckoned myself experienced. Maybe I was conceited – kidded myself I had survived so long partly because of good judgement in moments of crisis. When I came out to the Front I was an ignoramus, knew nothing and readily accepted established customs; now as a veteran I sometimes stuck out my neck, challenged Authority.

119

While collecting witnesses to appear before the Court, a sergeant told me he found the accused hiding in the ruins of a church (a church as sanctuary in the 20th century!). He knew Private Rogers personally, came from the same village near Bolton, the whole family was barmy, both parents in lunatic asylums, sister committed suicide. 'Can you swear that?' I asked.

'Police at Bolton would confirm, sir.'

When I presented evidence to the Court, after the irrefutable items, I suggested this possible evidence of sub-normality. The President said it couldn't be considered, was hearsay, would take too long to get a police report. That's when I stuck out my neck, 'With due respect, sir, I as Prosecutor feel it may be valid evidence.' One member, a captain, interposed, 'Nonsense. When this fellow enlisted, must have had a medical, was Al then. Only evidence now valid relates to his desertion.'

The other two members agreed. The President said to me condescendingly, 'I'm sure you understand that as Prosecutor you do not take part in the discussions of the Court.' He added, 'Members of the Court are always officers of experience.'

That riled me. Inwardly I cried – experience is found in front line trenches; which of you old men has more than I? With what I hoped was ironic humility, I replied to the President. 'Of course, sir, I appreciate the officers of a Court-Martial have great experience. I've been in the trenches for a year, I'm afraid I've forgotten my study of *The Manual of Military Law*. I didn't intend to exceed my duty as Prosecutor. I only suggested evidence the Court might wish to consider before passing a death sentence.'

They looked at one another and spoke together in under-tones. At last the President said, 'It's not denied you have a right to make the suggestion, but we are agreed it would necessitate an adjournment of the trial till the police have reported. In war, as I'm sure you know, quick decisions and prompt action are desirable.'

'Yes, sir.' I agreed at once.

'Very sensible of you. You consent then to withdraw the suggestion?'

'Yes of course, sir. No doubt your report will make it clear that the Prosecutor mentioned possible evidence of sub-normality in the accused, but that the evidence was not considered by the Court to be valid . . . something to that effect, sir, just to safeguard me if the matter ever came up again.' They all stared in astonishment. I added, 'Most likely sir, but I have in mind possible complications with Civil Law – insurance, in-heritance, that sort of complication. In Alderney I had a murder in my unit and Military Law got involved with Civil Law.'

The President stood up. 'We cannot make any reservations in our report. The Court will have to adjourn.'

Stuck out my neck to what purpose? The half-wit was probably tried by another court with no conceited young Prosecutor to prolong his miserable life. My inner mind (that chap with whom I spend so much time in silent conversation) claimed I'd 'made a stand' for some principle, but having seen so many sensible men die, wits and all, I concluded there wasn't likely to be any principle which would save a half-wit.

About this time, I first heard the diagnosis 'shell-shock'. Officers were found sometimes wandering away from their unit, or 'going down' as casualties, the expression 'going down' being in common use to mean leaving the front line for any reason. Officers could not be suspected of desertion; MOs invented the diagnosis 'shell-shock' which passed into current use. I first noted the expression in early summer 1917 – 'Padre goes down with shell-shock.'

A few days after this last Court-Martial I narrowly escaped

involvement in a case of Self-Inflicted Wound; a crime almost as serious as desertion, punished by a long sentence of hard labour in an English gaol. A desperate man might put his hand over the muzzle of a rifle and shoot off his trigger-finger, reckoning years in prison better than any longer in the front line. One night a lance-corporal named Hapson (commonly called Happy) came to me, a Very-Light pistol in one hand, the other hand in a bloody bandage.

'Accident, sir,' he reported. 'saw a movement beyond the wire, put up a Very-Light urgently, didn't get this hand clear in time.' He lifted the bandage to show a hand coated with black soot and blood. Half the palm was shot away.

He was very shaken, knew it looked like a Self-Inflicted. 'Pistol must be defective, sir; went off before I'd pressed the trigger.'

'Your hand wants attention at once. Get a stretcher-bearer to go with you to the MO. Leave the pistol with me.'

I trusted Hapson absolutely. Twice I had picked him to accompany me on patrol into No-Man's-Land. I examined the Very-Light pistol – mechanism seemed all right, trigger action normal. Was it defective? I didn't think so. Must be an accident, careless certainly; but aren't we all careless sometimes? I thought about the matter for several minutes. The MO would patch up Hapson, put him to sleep probably, and certainly report to Battalion HQ – 'a possible Self-Inflicted'. I should speak up for Hapson, but it looked like a Court-Martial case, and the decisive evidence would be an armourer's report on the pistol. I pictured Lance-Corporal Hapson disgraced, sent back to Blighty under military police escort to do ten years hard labour with one good hand.

No matter what discretion whispered, I told my inner man, I knew what I was going to *do*. I took the pistol and flung it as far as I could into No-Man's-Land. I put the evidence where it wouldn't be found in the dark, and where no one could search for it in daylight. So I took the law into my own hands, circumvented authority. I knew there'd be a row. There was. The Adjutant came from HQ to see me. The CO thought Lance-Corporal Hapson ought to face a Court-Martial, the pistol was essential evidence. 'Let's hope it *is* defective.' the Adjutant said. I told him what I'd done.

'Threw it into No-Man's-Land?' he exclaimed incredulously, giving me a searching look. 'What a damned fool thing to do.'

'It did occur to me to test the pistol by firing it again, sir, but I didn't fancy taking that risk myself, and I never ask any man to do what I'm not prepared to do myself, especially anything risky.' This Sandhurst cliché brought the beginning of a grin to his lips, so I added boldly, 'I thought it damned foolish to have a Very-Light pistol which had wounded one man available for anyone to pick up and use again.'

He nodded and smiled. 'Speculation on your part. All the same what you *did* was damned foolish. Don't know what the CO will think. No evidence ... no Court-Martial, I guess. Seems like Lance-Corporal Hapson's a lucky man.'

Like Lance Corporal Hapson, a Very-Light pistol was nearly my undoing. When I came out in 1916 the Germans had unquestioned superiority in aircraft. I saw captive balloons just behind our front line, anchored to the ground, looking like giant ugly slugs asleep in the clouds, each with a basket for two observers who kept watch over enemy trenches. German planes attacked these balloons. I saw several shot down in flames and the observers machine gunned as they parachuted to earth. Enemy planes were used mainly for reconnaissance, flying low over our trenches to keep an eye on possible movements. Almost every day one or more of these planes flew over, machine gunning with impunity, occasionally dropping bombs. Always when our planes tried to intervene they were driven off or shot down. As we were in trenches the machine gun fire wasn't much worry and the bombs were nothing like so bad as shells or minenwefers, but the visible evidence of Bosche superiority, day by day, week by week was serious for morale. Later when the odds were not so heavily against us duels took place over No-Man's-Land between individual pilots who became aces like film stars, so that our men bet on them.

The increase in numbers of aircraft extended the area of the war: they could bomb almost any distance from the trench system, in contrast to the limited range of artillery. This new factor had to be remembered when troops moved any distance: we were liable to be bombed, though in fact it seldom happened. On one occasion the whole of our division was withdrawn from trenches to reorganise and recuperate. Then I perpetrated a gaffe so daft as to be almost beyond belief. When we left the front line I received from the incoming unit a Handing Over Certificate of stores – 11,000 rounds of small arms ammunition, 1,200 hand-bombs and various small items including 4 Very-Light pistols. As I led my platoon down the communication trench on the start of our long trek to the Divisional Rest Centre I stepped on something hard and picked it out of the mud – a Very-Light pistol. These pistols were always going stray and a buckshee one was worth having even when covered with mud. It was a dark night so without any close examination I stuffed it into the left side pocket of my Burberry. In winter I wore a Trench Coat but in summer a Burberry, day and night, wet or fine, hot or cold, and always I reserved the right side pocket for my pistol, loaded of course, in an open holster. Any time that I woke from sleep my right hand automatically felt for the pistol while my left hand sought my gas helmet to make certain I had the two things essential for life.

The Divisional Rest Centre was in a woodland camp, the men to sleep on the ground which was dry under the trees, and the officers sharing a row of Bell tents, four to a tent. I was tired but generally very satisfied with the prospect of several uninterrupted nights' sleep. I waited till the Cookhouse made tea for the men and then joined my three companions in our tent. We grumbled about this and that as exhausted men do. It was too cold to undress but I spread my Burberry over my blanket. When I was almost asleep I felt something uncomfortably heavy on me and sat up to investigate. To my astonishment it was the mud-covered Very-Pistol, the mud now dry. My mind was blank, too tired for thought, but automatically my fingers began to pick off the dry mud. When the muzzle was more or less clear of mud I pressed the trigger. My gaffe – I hadn't looked to see if the pistol was loaded.

The Very-Light shot across the tent missing the head of one of my comrades. If it had hit him he'd have fallen dead. It made a neat round hole in the canvas of the tent, rose high and for a moment hung above the tree tops casting a brilliant illumination far and wide before slowly parachuting to the ground.

My tent companions were aghast – what a thing to do! If a German plane had been anywhere near he'd have spotted us and called up all the planes in the area to bomb us to bits. Naturally the whole camp was roused. My confusion was complete. I saw and heard the tent surrounded, everyone talking, the Adjutant amongst them. He asked questions, seemed to think there must be a reasonable explanation, but at last went away saying he would report to the CO. I am naturally cautious, always imagining possible troubles, not expecting them but aware of the possibility. I kept on telling myself so but that didn't account for this extraordinary gaffe. The next I remember was someone shouting, 'The CO wants you – at once.'

He regarded me seriously, 'You all right?'

'Yes sir. I'm very sorry. I just can't understand . . .'

'Not shell-shock?', he interrupted.

'Oh, no sir. I'm very fit . . . can't understand . . .'

'One of those things which can never be understood. Lucky there were no Bosche aircraft about. And lucky for you' that you have a sound reputation.'

In a coal-mining district not far from the city of Lens, was a prominent feature of the landscape known as The Double Crassier.

On the back of trench maps a Glossary listed French words with their English translations – *arbre isolé* an isolated tree, *fosse* a pit, and *crassier* a slag-heap. Sometimes the languages got mixed, as in *Bois de Ploegsteert*, where the large forest had printed within its acres Hyde Park Corner and Mud Lane and Three Huns Farm and Dead Horse Corner.

The Double Crassier was two adjacent slag-heaps which ran at right angles across No-Man's-Land, a distance of about one hundred yards beginning at ground level just within the German line and rising in height till they ended abruptly at sixty feet almost over our trench. A narrow trench along the top of one Crassier gave the enemy an observation post from which he could look right down into our trench. We countered this advantage with a kind of 'stairway' trench of one hundred steps from our front line to the top of the Crassier, with a short cross trench to give us a wide view of No-Man's Land. In that trench we were only a few yards from the enemy. I spent a good part of every day up on the Crassier in our short trench: it was fascinating to hear Germans talking to one another – for me a kind of eaves-dropping on another world. Exceptional precautions were necessary: 'Lieut. Brown informed me that our SOS is now RED but a Captain Robinson came round later and

The Double Crassier

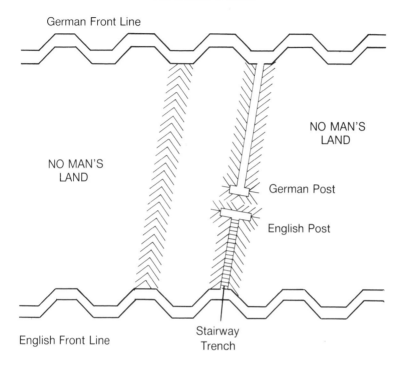

German Front Line

NO MAN'S
LAND

NO MAN'S
LAND

German Post

English Post

English Front Line

Stairway
Trench

told me it was GREEN. Can you let me know which is correct? Till I hear from you I shall use RED.' I wrote this message to Company HQ in a Field Message Book, which I still have with the carbon copies intact. Next day I wrote another message, 'I have RED bulb in lamp as ordered. Please let me know password for tonight.' Passwords (changed every night) were customary but SOS lamps and flags were exceptional precautions to alert HQ because of the proximity of the front lines. At any time night or day we, or the enemy, could have lobbed bombs over the sand bags between us or made an overwhelming attack.

I never understood some slang words used by my men but one which came from India – cushy – was probably English soldiers' corruption of a Hindustani word meaning safety. The PBI used 'cushy' in varied ways, as though it were poetic – a safe job at the Base was cushy (always intended in contempt), and so was any trench or front-line duty which was not especially dangerous: it was used almost as an encouragement. An incoming unit would ask, 'What's this trench like?' and would almost certainly get a comforting reply, 'Cushy, old man' – even if it wasn't! There were cushy trenches certainly, in areas where No-Man's-Land was exceptionally wide. I should have dubbed our trench on The Double Crassier as cushy because we and Jerry both had advantages which might have been lost by any overt hostility.

One day the Adjutant phoned me on an ordinary RE line. He was boiling over with indignation: a civilian had turned up with a letter from 'some damned politician' asking to be shown the front line so that he could write a newspaper article. War Correspondents were unknown at that date – at least unknown to the PBI. 'Damned irregular, encouraging a pen-pusher to dabble in military matters,' snorted the Adjutant. I was to show this fellow The Double Crassier, 'it's cushy enough in daylight,' thought the Adjutant. I grumbled about this chore to the officer in the next platoon, a chap named Selstone. He was sympathetic, 'Take this Press-Wallah half-a-dozen times up and down your 'stairway' trench, Old Man; if that doesn't kill him it'll give him enough to write home about.' Then Selstone suggested a joke, a leg-pull, a brain-wave I thought, and so it proved to be.

Instead of showing the journalist The Double Crassier we took him to an extensive ruin about a kilometre behind the lines, a ruin commonly called the Folly. It had been a factory, destroyed early in the war, nothing left standing, only basement passages and below-ground vaults partly blocked by rubble. Called the Folly because at a time when everyone had the wind-up expecting a Big Push by the Bosche a Staff-Officer tried to make the ruins a reserve stronghold. PBI working parties had spent many nights filling sandbags for gun emplacements before it dawned on Division Headquarters that the place was much too near the trench system and would be blown to smithereens before an attack began. The project was abandoned and PBI laughed at the Staff-Officer, calling the ruins his Folly. Now the place was deserted, no one went there and it was never shelled.

Pulling the leg of a credulous journalist proved to be good fun. He turned up wearing a steel helmet and with a gas mask. 'I want to know everything,' he said, notebook in hand. Selstone, who came with me, told him the Folly was part of the front line and anything but cushy, 'We must crawl here, hands and knees, parapet badly knocked about last week, two chaps killed, several wounded.' To me Selstone added, 'Have you heard if those Essex men died?' Before I realised this was part of the leg-pull he cried, 'For God's sake keep low.' Our visitor wasn't used to crawling about in rubble and was soon out of breath. 'Another hundred yards', suggested Selstone hopefully, 'if those five-nines an hour ago were not direct hits we ought to be able to rest in one of the deep dugouts.' Of course there weren't any dugouts, only stinking vaults that had once stored chemicals. I think we crawled a good kilometre in the ruins before the journalist asked, 'Anywhere safe for us to sit a bit?'

Selstone and I vied with each other telling tall stories of trench life, our victim jotting down names like Hell-fire Ditch, Minenwerfer and Crassier. I pretended to hear distant gunfire, 'Might be only a pip-squeak or perhaps shrapnel,' I hazarded, 'but we'd better lie alongside the remains of that steam-boiler.' Selstone went one better, he sat up suddenly swearing he'd heard the peculiar dull explosion of a gas shell. He made the journalist take his gas mask from its case, 'Probably one of those hydrocyanide gas shells the Hun just started using, no warning smell, one sniff fatal.' He volunteered to climb up to ground level to investigate but the newspaper chap pleaded with him not to take such risk. 'Not on my account,' he said bravely. When we reached the part of Folly ruin where one could see The Double Crassier I explained, 'Looks a long way off but really quite near, it is part of this front line and only a few feet from the Bosche.' My colleague added, 'Don't talk too loudly, better whisper, our voices could be picked up on one of those clever German instruments.'

When the journalist had gone the story of our little folly spread through the battalion, but the real joke came a fortnight later in a London daily newspaper – the writer had been in the front line, under shell fire and the threat of snipers. It was entitled, *The Sinister Double Crassier*.

One of our Generals issued to all subalterns a pamphlet, *Questions a Platoon Commander should ask Himself*. Some of these questions were worth attention, though to be sure written by a High-Up who'd probably never seen a trench: but the first asked in bold type, 'Am I as offensive as I might be?' In every mess the question was tossed about with hilarity – 'Are you . . . was he . . . shall we be . . . ?' and so on. *The New Church Times*, printed in a cellar dug-out, had a gorgeous picture of an offensive subaltern wearing fancy items of uniform then becoming fashionable, replacing the drab official uniform of pre-war years. Amongst the PBI, 'Am I as offensive as I might be?' was probably the best joke of the war. But it was just as well that its author never got to hear of the live-and-let-live on the top of the Double Crassier.

I am confident my Victorian grandparents never said 'Damn' and my father was even more extreme: he winced when anyone took the name of the Almighty in vain. At school I learned 'Damn' and 'Blast' (not to be taken home, or spoken aloud, only to repeat in the silence of my mind) but I was a generation and many miles away from ancestors, in another country. Had I not, on a piece of string around my neck, the Disc issued at Southampton declaring that I was an individual, unique amongst the millions of men involved in this war? The string was a little grubby (string being a rare commodity in trenches) but after months at the Front I was still proud of my Identity Disc, as though it were a medal awarded for an heroic deed.

When I joined the army I was shocked to hear 'Damn' and 'Blast' used so frequently in the Officers' Mess. Men in trenches didn't seem to use these words. My men were bilingual, amongst themselves using a language to which I only understood a few words and when talking to officers switching to what they called 'pukka talk'. Some of their words I suspected to be indecent – the sort dictionaries avoid as 'not used in polite society'. One word in particular used by my men as noun, verb or adjective worried me. I was, indeed, a little afraid of it, maybe the discovery of its meaning would only embarrass me. Partial enlightenment came at a church parade.

I don't know who ordered the church parades when we came out on Rest. During my first eight months we had ten, but only three in seven months of 1917. I liked these parades, they were simple, no rituals or theology, only hymns, a lesson read from the Bible and a short address by the Chaplain. (In the front line we had no religion – that is, no church parades, no regular visits from our Chaplain.) The men were indifferent though most sang the hymns, probably to words other than those printed in the hymn books. We used three hymn books, blue, yellow and green, the hymns differently numbered – the Chaplain announced the first line and then added the hymn number in all three books. The men gambled on whether a hymn would have the same number in two books and, of course, the usual end-of-the-war superstition – that when the chosen hymn had the same number in all three books the war would end!

In an open meadow with a wall down one side against which
many of the men dozed, hungry for sleep after an all-night trek
from the front line, we sang *Fight the Good Fight* (63 in the blue
book, 41 in the yellow and 82 in the green) but not very heartily.
The Chaplain then said, 'Instead of my address, General
Pawson will speak to you.' He turned to a little man, sitting in a
real chair beside him and said, 'We are honoured by the
presence at our service of the Commander of this Division. He
has a special message for us.' I had not seen the Divisional
Commander before and when he stood up I was surprised
how insignificant he looked. But his voice was loud and
piercing.

'I asked your Chaplain for this opportunity to address you on
a religious occasion, a church parade, because in your regiment
there are men possessed by an unclean spirit. I need not repeat
the disgusting word many of you utter every time you speak.
This unclean spirit must be cast out. I will not allow it in my
Division. Here you have not the refining influence of women,
you think it doesn't matter to speak filth which you would not
speak in the presence of your wives and daughters – and so you
have allowed this foul word to possess you.' I listened to
General Pawson with astonishment, expecting enlightenment:
at last I should learn the meaning of this over-worked word.
The Divisional Commander told us we should be proud of the
regiment's history, reminded us of our Battle Honours – the
Crimea, Indian Mutiny, South Africa and a lot more – even
told us that some General in the Crimean War said the 64th
Foot 'was a thin red line tipped with steel'. Being keen on
poetry I liked that metaphor, 'tipped with steel', but what
could my men make of this tirade? Glancing round I saw many
were asleep and, anyway, they never listened to the Chaplain's
address. Why should they care what this pipsqueak loud-
voiced man thought about them? I began to resent it on their

behalf. After more talk about the brave men in the past who built up an honourable reputation which must not be defiled the Divisional Commander concluded, 'I tell you again this indecent word is not to be used any longer. It is so common amongst you that it has become the shameful nickname by which your battalion is known throughout my Division . . . I won't allow it . . . it is a disgrace to the whole Division.'

I could hardly believe what I heard. This condemnation of my men turned my first resentment to bitter indignation. General Pawson, instead of returning to his chair for the rest of the service walked off abruptly, absent-mindedly carrying away in his hand a yellow hymn book.

Gosh! I became livid – that pipsqueak thinks he's God Almighty. My men may be foul-mouthed, may use an indecent word (which I still don't understand) but I've lived alongside them, shared Life with them, been with them in many a strafe, crawled with some in No-Man's-Land, been over the top with them on the Somme, soon to go over the top with them again; and that old Dud who has never faced such ordeals says they are a disgrace to his Division!

When the last hymn was announced some of the chaps near me began to stir, awakened by their subconscious alarm clocks. I heard one ask, 'What was that bugger gassing about?' And the reply came, 'Buggered if I know, I was having a kip. Where's the old bugger gone now?'

CHAPTER NINE

Second Leave
and a Crooked Corner

I was granted a second leave after I had been out thirteen months – to start next day at Dawn-Stand-To. At almost the last minute an order came from Division – a patrol to report on an uncertain situation where the enemy had pushed forward east of Hellfire Corner and south of Hooge. I knew that area better than anyone in our battalion, so notwithstanding my pending leave this tricky patrol was allotted to me: a starlight night, no moon, trekking over shell-torn country, crawling in Zouave Wood and Sanctuary Wood. When I got away at dawn I thanked my lucky stars (almost a convert to the mumbo-jumbo of astrology).

My first leave had plunged me back into the delights of home life little changed from my childhood, familiar habits persisting in spite of war. My second leave found home life very different – my elder sister doing war work on a farm, her bedroom occupied by a girl medical student. My father explained, 'Your mother needs distraction to keep her mind from anxieties. We were asked to make a home for this girl student who comes from Birmingham. A nice girl, considerate and brings other students to the house. Your mother is often quite busy in the evenings, preparing supper for them.'

My father needed distractions too. Always an adult to me, now an old man (my generation invented the phrase, 'too old at forty'). He was so old I couldn't hide a smile when he told me with gravity he was going to enlist in the army, 'Casualties so much greater than ever expected . . . I must do my bit.'

'War is fought in trenches, Dad, nowhere else. It will be won or lost in the front line. You're far too old for anything but a cushy job.' I tried to persuade him not to do anything yet . . . told him the war couldn't last much longer, and laughingly sang him a song popular with the men, *Oh my! I don't want to die, I want to go home.* At first he wasn't convinced, so I told him that even some officers talked lightly of starting what signaller's jargon called PIP ACK ACK PIP, an abbreviation for Peace-at-any-Price. 'Not serious, of course. It comes from this American talk of a negotiated peace instead of unconditional surrender.'

He shook his head as one who fears a joke may become serious, but he concluded, 'We must pray for an early honourable peace – whatever that means.'

I told him I'd been to Mill Cemetery at Vlamertinghe twice in the month before my leave. Our grave was properly looked after. He seemed very relieved and hurried away to tell my mother. But when he came back I talked of Toc H and their slogan 'All rank abandon ye who enter here'; for I knew in politics father was a strong advocate of democratic equality. He responded by telling me of a nurse named Cavell, a woman of fifty, shot by Germans for helping English prisoners to escape. She said at her execution *patriotism is not enough*; a revolutionary idea but thinking about it I knew the old nurse was right. We who volunteered to fight for King and Country were patriots, bursting with sentiment, but three years of war had dried up patriotism. There were no more Englishmen willing to fight. Men were conscripts now, dragged by Law from their homes. I had seen some, come out to our battalion shortly before my leave.

Another custom which I had grown up to accept as common to almost all families since the dawn of Christianity – family prayers before breakfast – was now discontinued. I didn't like to ask why but my father told me, 'Only one of you children at home; and she's a lazy girl, often late getting up, family prayers seem somehow forlorn.'

It was the done thing for officers on leave to visit their old school – vanity I suppose, showing oneself as quite grown up, and moreover a kind of credit to the school. The Head talked to me as to an equal and explained his problem of finding new masters: one who answered an advertisement had excellent qualifications but turned out to be a Quaker! The Latin master, a bogey-man to me when I hadn't done my prep, was now patronising. 'We never forget you men out at the front doing your bit . . . let me see . . . two years since you left . . . Don't tell me your name . . . it'll come to me in a moment. As Cicero put it, *memoria est thesaurus omnium rerum et custos*, memory is the treasury and guardian of everything.'

'Afraid I wasn't much good at Latin, sir,' I said.

'Too many of you with that distinction . . . but don't tell me . . . I never forget names . . . it'll come in a moment . . . Ah, yes, got it . . . Dobson, of course.' He wasn't really concerned with me, only wanted to show off his memory. The other masters were much the same, patronising but not interested in our army life, no questions about trenches or war: all turned back as soon as possible to the subjects they taught, facts which must not be disturbed by the clamour of war. They were learned men in their profession, grammar school standard, but, I reflected, without any conception of reality; extinct volcanoes. We who live under the shadow of death sometimes see light, they dwell always in the shadow of blackout curtains and see no light at all. They pass on their ignorance to future generations.

This shying away from what I supposed was the greatest event in the long history of *homo sapiens* seemed widespread. As I moved about amongst civilians, met the elderly friends of my parents, I was often acclaimed a hero (in front-line trenches the word means nothing). More than once strangers patted me on the back and offered to give me a drink in a pub; but even these good-natured people did not want to learn how heroes live and die. Exceptionally, I was asked, 'Do the French women who wash your clothes also mend them?' and a man said, 'When it's too dark to go on fighting – are you free for the evening, can you get to a cinema?'

Of course, war had brought personal loss to some – husbands, fathers, lovers, sons (to be mourned in customary conventions), but the talk I heard was of rations, shortage of luxuries, taxes, savings, highly paid munition workers and profiteers. Victory was taken to be inevitable, followed by a quick return to pre-war security – law and order, hang the Kaiser and make the Germans pay. In a warm bed after the luxury of a hot bath, I could not but contrast the two standards – war as I'd experienced it for a year and peace in England. Once or twice I caught myself thinking ahead, beyond the few more days of leave: an uncertain future discouraged daydreams, forced me to live in the present, very strictly the present. I felt the past was gone; real life was only in the present, all else fantasy.

This second leave would have been gloomy but for the girl Medical living in the house and her student friends. I was shy of girls, perhaps because I had two sisters. Civilians at home imagined we often saw French girls: the men stationed at base camps and behind the Front probably did, but not PBI in trenches. I'd hardly seen a French girl in twelve months, which no doubt influenced my reaction when I met the girl students who now came to our house. They reckoned me a war-hero. (Glory-War, of course, how could they know anything of real War?) On the Saturday before I returned to France someone organised a party, an old-fashioned entertain-yourselves party:

songs round the piano, guessing games, charades and after supper an uproarious hide-and-seek all round the house in the dark. That evening I escaped the thrall of shyness, because we all seemed to be acting in a play. Looking round for somewhere to hide I remembered a big round basket on the landing upstairs which I sometimes used when I was a child: a bamboo thing brought by one of my uncles from India. I took off the lid and swung a leg over to get in. To my surprise there was a giggle and a gasped protest, 'I've bagged this, you're too late.'

'Who are you?' I demanded, thinking I recognised the voice of our Medical.

'Mind my hair, such a caboodle doing it in a bun.'

'Tell me who you are.'

'Never you mind, this is my place to hide, take your hand from my head.'

'First tell me your name.'

'Cleopatra,' whispered with a giggle.

'Silly! Tell me your real name.'

'Oh! all right – Helen of Troy, and you've ruined my hair.'

'Cheeky; for that I'll jolly well pull your bun down.'

But I didn't. I heard someone creeping upstairs. 'Someone coming,' I whispered, 'I'm off, good luck.' I put the lid back, moved along the landing and allowed myself to be caught. She wasn't our Medical, but a girl I didn't know. Afterwards she told everyone she'd found a wizard place to hide but a horrid man tried to take it. 'I had to push him out,' she declared, 'but see what's happened to my hair.' She patted her head and looked towards me grinning. I laughed; for a shy man I reckoned I'd been bold. I was pleased with this childish gallantry, talking to a strange girl as I might have spoken to one of my sisters!

My parents were an anxiety. I realised now that my brother and I between us had caused my mother daily apprehension for eighteen months, always watching fearfully for a telegraph boy at the front door with a War Office telegram. I found myself telling my father that the Germans were not the only people responsible for the war. We should have to live with them and other nations when peace came. Men and women of his generation didn't realise how the world was being changed. 'I'm sure you're right,' he said, 'We look back to the greatness of the last century with pride, we criticise everything new.'

'Ever been to a cinema?' I asked. 'They are opening up everywhere.'

'I've not seen a moving picture; but shouldn't it be pronounced *Kinema*, from the Greek?'

'Name doesn't matter. It's the picture which counts. The Charlie Chaplin film on in Princes Street now is sure to be funny. Let me take you and mother, make her laugh, cheer her up no end.'

I thought the film very funny. My father said, 'An interesting experience. Kinemas could be used in education I expect.' My mother said, 'Don't think we didn't enjoy it, darling, think only that we feel your love in taking us.' Well, it was a failure, of course. I had another idea. From the beginning of the war, officers and other volunteers, as soon as they had a uniform, got their photographs taken professionally, expensive cabinet portraits to display on a mantelpiece at home. I'd been pleased to see mine alongside my brother's in his Artists' Rifles uniform, now joined by my sister in Land Army uniform. Vanity, all is vanity, but as I looked at the three of us children always staring into the sitting room, every day and all day, I thought my mother might be distracted by having her photo taken! 'Nonsense,' she protested, 'I'm an old woman.' 'But it's for *me*,' I said. 'I've only that snapshot I took with my five-bob Kodak. I want a proper photograph to take back with me.' I kept on talking lest she began to wonder, as I did, what on earth I should do with a cabinet portrait and no mantelpiece – stick it up in a dug-out? She wouldn't know that many dug-outs displayed pictures from French magazines of half-dressed girls, some less than half-dressed. At last I persuaded her. The result was a flop; in the portrait she looked indescribably miserable.

The dread day of farewell came. I suggested to my father it would be better if they didn't see me off at Waverley Station. He replied very gently that he'd already put it to my mother, and she had said, 'I won't disgrace anyone. I must see the last of my boy.' She did her best, but when the guard came from his van, whistle in hand, she wept. 'Haven't you done your bit? Couldn't you ask them to bring you home to teach new recruits at a training camp in England?' (My poor mother, *me* to wangle a cushy job, *me* to be a scrimshanker?) I put an arm round her shaking shoulders, aware that the gesture could be but threadbare comfort. I couldn't find any words. There is a Chinese saying, 'to help a heart round a corner'. That's what I had been trying to do – help my mother's almost broken heart round a crooked corner. And I knew I had failed.

I brought back from my second leave a state of depression new to me. Over a year in trenches, so concerned with my own affairs, I had not realised the strain of war on my parents. Now it was too late. On the long train journey to London and Folkestone I thought of my friends: school friendships ended by war, some dead, some disabled, the rest scattered. Army friendships? Yes, and very real, but fleeting; perhaps only Hardy and Watson could be lasting.

My mother's suggestion of a cushy job in Blighty started me wondering how much longer my nerves would hold out. An officer's duties and concern for his men took the edge off his own fears; we were actors in a play, every time we listened to an approaching shell we screened our nerves by acting an entirely imaginary character – the fearless man. I'd known brave men gradually lose their nerves till they couldn't play this tragedy any longer, dared not leave a dug-out to perform duties: one chap, a captain, ended it with suicide. How long did I have to keep up the rôle? I couldn't expect a third leave.

I rejoined my battalion near Dickebusch and at 3 a.m. on 7th June, from near Scottish Wood, saw Hill 60 blown sky-high by mines, a very spectacular show. For weeks I had known our Royal Engineers were excavating below Hill 60 – not much of a hill (I suppose only 60 metres above sea-level) but it commanded a view across the low-lying Ypres salient and was held tenaciously by the enemy. My front trench opposite Hill 60 was visited periodically by two or three furtive Sappers who disappeared down a hole carrying paraphenalia for their mole-like activities. The RE captain consulted me about places to dump the earth they brought up, places where it wouldn't be noticed by the Bosche, like disused saps, old latrines or exceptional shell holes. I used to pull his leg about the folly of so much waste effort – was he making a route through the Earth for Australians to come to the Western Front avoiding U-boats? Before I went on leave he told me the mine was almost under Hill 60. 'I'll tip you off when we are about to light the fuse, worth watching, nothing like it before, ever.' Indeed, a strange way of making war. One moment a hill (small but complete, as it was established at God's creation), next moment gone, nothing there any more, not enough to show a hump on the skyline. For me, however, it was stimulating, gave my mind a new experience to think about, lifted my depression. During the next week my records illustrate how varied my days became; 'very hot . . . busy burying Huns . . . heavy shelling . . . Adjutant wounded . . . eight officers killed . . . to Poperinghe for a bath . . . Mother and Father's Wedding Day . . . badly shelled with new German high-velocity gun which our men call Wipers Express, twenty

to thirty casualties from a single shell, Colonel killed . . . lazy
day . . . Major Cotton killed, the MO and a subaltern
wounded.'

How often long-expected news takes one by surprise! Talk of
an impending Big Push was a common rumour. My friend
Watson brought it alive. 'Listen,' he said in a confidential
voice, 'What I'm telling you is a top secret, don't breathe a hint
of it to anyone. The battalion is to be withdrawn from trenches
and sent back to an inhabited farming area to rehearse for going
over the top. Can't tell you the date, but when it happens I, as
Intelligence Officer, have a special job. Of course I don't go
over the top with you chaps, but a direction-tape has to be put
out in No-Man's-Land an hour or so before the attack starts so
that the men advance directly towards the objective – means
compass readings in the dark, and someone to work with me.
The new CO hasn't had time yet to know anyone, so he's
leaving me to find my partner. I want you; if you'll take on the
job . . . shouldn't need more than ten to twenty minutes on our
edge of No-Man's-Land . . . a risk of course, but nothing like an
ordinary patrol.' He waited for me to speak. Of course I should
do it, felt proud at being asked, but this news was all such a
surprise. He threw in a final comment. 'The big show will start
3 a.m. one morning about a fortnight from now. Your men will
find the time of waiting – while we two are playing about with
tape – rather tense. We can fix details so you will be with them
then. I'd like to tell the CO now that you are willing to help me
with the tape.'

So the Big Push became more than a rumour; was indeed
imminent. As I went about the usual duties I told myself, and
repeated it again and again, that I was actually involved now in
preparations for a real Big Push. How the future would work
out was beyond imagination, but I should have plenty to do, no
time for doubts or apprehensions.

Naturally Watson asked about my leave – what are civilian rations like now? Are there still luxuries which rich people can buy? Enough fuel for one hot bath a week? Is water rationed? Is clothes-rationing equitable? Had I been in London, seen any shows? *Chu Chin Chow* was said to be all the rage.

I told my friend I'd had a good leave, no shortages of food and more variety than army rations; my family had cold baths during my week at home so I could use their allowance of hot. But I confessed that I came away dispirited. The university students I met were a jolly lot but life was grim for my parents, too old to cope with war, too set in their ways. I mentioned my mother's idea of a cushy job, which naturally I didn't take seriously, but it had set me wondering if I was getting a bit windy and how long I should last. Watson laughed, as though discounting any such notion. 'Nonsense, old man!' but his next remark suggested he didn't think it quite nonsense. With some hesitation he gave me another piece of confidential news, 'Don't tell anyone, but *I've* applied for a cushy job! The army is beginning to take Intelligence seriously, not of course at battalion level but there's a Staff Officer appointment coming up at Division. I should like the work, much more scope than here. So I've applied, and I'm to move to Division in about six weeks. I feel a bit of a scrimshanker but it's the scope of Intelligence work that interests me.' I knew I should miss Watson and said so. He nodded, 'Well, I've told you my news, because when I go you might take my place as Battalion IO. Easy for me to put your name forward tactfully and at the right time. CO is sure to agree.'

A very welcome prospect for me – live at HQ instead of the front trench, not such anxious responsibilities, no long periods of routine duty, a good deal less shelling, out of range of 'minnies' and machine gun fire. Watson said, 'Not cushy; in fact sometimes a bit hazardous like this tape in No-Man's-

Land, though that's exceptional. One advantage for you, opportunities for long spells of shut-eye.'

'A new lease of life,' I said.

He nodded. 'Keep it to yourself, at present mum's the word.'

To my delight my old friend Hardy rejoined the battalion, Hardy who had been my nursemaid when I arrived in the front line all innocent. After months in hospital in Blighty he'd been at the Regimental Depot doing a clerical job. From time to time medical boards had moved him from C3 towards A1. When he realised the possibility of being sent out again he was tempted to 'wangle a cushy' – as he expressed it to me. There were good opportunities to do so at the Depot, but remembering our scorn of scrimshankers he let matters take their course and here he was back with the battalion just in time for the Big Push. He looked older and more grave. I scarely knew him as the mentor who helped me so much when I first came out, but he exercised the same pungent criticism of the high command. He was posted to A Company, and in the pressure of our 'over-the-top' preparations I only had one good talk with him. He spoke as though at the Depot everyone knew more about the Big Push than we did, which might well be.

'Mustn't shake anyone's morale,' he said, 'but between ourselves Flanders is waterlogged from near a month of rain. Too much to expect Brass Hats to know that will create problems bringing up supplies.' He went on to suggest that Staff Officers base their plans on statistics and averages which don't allow any consideration of locale or weather. 'When artillery have churned up a few square kilometres of earth into a sea of mud, GHQ will send in the Tanks,' he said sarcastically, allowing himself to imagine fantastic developments, 'The Tanks will sink. The WO will then have a brilliant idea, issue PBI with *Wings, Water, mark IA, infantry for the use of,* and expect us to rescue Tank Corps chaps from their sunken craft. Journalists already call the Tanks 'land ships'. So the politicians will take the initiative next, and put the Tank Corps under Admiralty instead of WO.' 'Chaps at the Depot any idea how long the war is going on?' I asked.

'Brass Hats reckon Germans all starving, only want this Push to finish the war. They say prisoners we take will be so thin they can be marched down communication trenches four abreast. But most chaps at Depot think the war is stalemate, won't ever end.'

One day Watson showed me the new Trench Map to be issued to us for the Big Push. Printed by Ordnance Survey, Southampton, it was the first map I'd seen which gave names to all trenches, ours and the enemy's. Older maps gave a few names, such as farms and woods and the larger *étangs* (village ponds) and names given at various times by our men – Old Kent Road, Shrapnel Corner, Clapham Junction, Tower Hamlets and so on. The new map had names for every trench, hundreds of them; odd words without meaning as though taken from a dictionary but in groups, starting with a particular letter. For trenches in our possession the letter I (Imp Avenue, Illusive, Imperfect, Image Crescent, etc) and enemy trenches with letter J (Jehovah, Jordan, Jericho, Java etc). Watson murmured that we should be told our objectives in the official pow-wow to be given by the CO but he knew my company was to start from *Image Crescent* attacking *Jehovah* and then *Jordan* where another regiment would pass through to carry forward the attack to *Jericho*.

It was obvious from other parts of this map that no associated meanings were intended but, to my mind, the Biblical names at any rate did convey some suggestions.

Are the records in my pocket diary, written nearly seventy years ago, more accurate than my memories? When I began this fragment of autobiography I relied on memory and would have sworn the wise Chinese proverb, 'Pale ink is better than a good memory' did not apply in my case. But as I wrote I wanted to check a date and fished the diary from the bottom drawer of my desk where it had been unregarded for years. I was pleased to find how consistently the diary confirms memory, even in details. However there is an exception – an entry of six words, written on Monday 23rd June 1917, recording an event of which I have no recollection at all; reading it now is as surprising as when an odd coin drops from clothes which haven't been worn for a long time. The six words: 'lecture on the Battle of Verdun.'

Memory insists vehemently that I've never heard a lecture on Verdun. We English PBI hardly ever had any contact with the allies we ignorantly despised; to us Verdun was only a place in the French part of the Western Front where there had been heavy fighting, like our Battle of the Somme only of course not so important. Why should anyone lecture us on Verdun? But I'll never again doubt that Chinese proverb.

After this revelation I thought I had better consult French history. I learn that after Verdun a General named Nivelle proposed a new strategy which he claimed would end the Great War in a few days. Lloyd George was impressed and invited Nivelle to London to discuss strategy with Haig. It seems the two Generals met in England. Naturally we practical soldiers knew nothing about strategy or the goings-on of the War Cabinet, but the orders given us before we went over the top were somewhat on the lines proposed by Nivelle. Certainly I didn't listen to the lecture and I don't suppose anyone did for we distrusted information from official sources.

My memory let me down on the lecture but is quite clear about the event recorded next day, 'Address by Archbishop of Canterbury'. My ears may have listened to the Address, my mind didn't. Perhaps the Archbishop made a few notes of what he came to tell us, certainly he assumed someone would listen. I don't remember even his subject and I doubt if anyone in the battalion paid much attention – just another boost of morale. But significant – The Most Reverent His Grace the Lord Archbishop of Canterbury come all the way from Blighty to address us – us, a unit of the Poor Bloody Infantry withdrawn for a few days from trenches to rehearse for a Big Push. Why us? What had we done to be so honoured?

The Address made no impression on me, but I was thrilled to see an Archbishop; never seen one before. In Scotland the state Kirk (and in England the nonconformist churches) had no bishops, disapproved of such eccelesiastical authority, so I was prejudiced: but surely some respect must be due to a big gun like an Archbishop? I remember clearly how, as I watched his dignified performance with several attendant chaplains, my thoughts wandered amongst my war experiences – church parades, Toc H, Hardy's outbursts – all leading me to believe the war would inevitably bring changes in the established Church. Now I had doubts sufficient to stir again the disillusion I thought I'd overcome. What did Establishment leaders living in safety and comfort, know about war or any need for reconsidering beliefs? I saw, or thought I saw, why this Address had been laid on for us. Some Christians thought a man's salvation depended upon his dying in a state of Grace; confess and repent while there is time. The reality of Life and Death in trenches rendered this adage obsolete but maybe official church doctrine hadn't got there yet: we might need that state of grace before the week was out.

In bitterness I fancied the Archbishop back in Blighty, telling the House of Lords 'I've just returned from a visit to the Front . . . our boys in high spirits . . . won't be long before we have good news . . . very soon now.' What with a lecture on war strategy and the Archbishop's concern for our spiritual welfare something must be coming our way!

My diary entries for the rest of the week are – 'Wednesday, marched to Mic-Mac Camp, reconnoitred to Image Crescent. Thursday, bombed by aeroplanes. Friday, bombed by aeroplanes. Saturday, 1 a.m. gas shells at Mic-Mac.'

CHAPTER TEN

Over The Top

The Battle of the Somme enriched the English language with the phrase – 'going over the top'. Not slang: a clearly defined and planned military manoeuvre. After the war 'over the top' became a common metaphor meaning any 'dangerous activity', civil or military, often implying a more or less forlorn hope. As to the army use, trenches being below ground level gave infantry some protection from shells, machine gun fire and mortars. When an attack on the enemy was made, the infantry had to abandon their accustomed protection (such as it was) and climb over the top, to charge across No-Man's-Land. The military phrase covers more than just climbing over the top, it includes the whole operation up to the moment of personal combat on the far side of No-Man's-Land. Before the Somme we reckoned it a foolish risk even to take a quick glance above the trench level in daylight, so the order 'over the top' seemed indeed dangerous.

Now, a little more than a year after the Somme I was to lead my men over the top in the Big Push. At the centre of my mind was a conviction that in war things don't happen as planned, confusion is the order of every day, the real commander-in-chief is General Chaos.

Much later I read a comment on 'going over the top', in a letter written at this time by a young French soldier at Verdun, a stretcher-bearer named Teilhard de Chardin: 'The infantry man leaving his trench for the attack is a man apart, a man who has lived a minute of life of which other men have simply no conception at all . . . it is an exaltation accompanied by a certain pain, nevertheless it is indeed an exaltation.'

When de Chardin was world-famous as scientist, philosopher and religious teacher, his biographer, Robert Speight, said, 'the war was the matrix of his whole thinking about the nature of man and the universe.' I was no Teilhard de Chardin, never learned in science or philosophy, or in any degree distinguished, but in the impending Big Push I was to experience that minute of Life of which those who have not experienced it can have no conception at all.

When I was gazetted I didn't know the word pow-wow but I found it well-established in the army, in constant use, meaning any occasion when a senior officer makes a pronouncement. (Surprising and quite delightful when you come to think of it, pow-wow being a Red Indian word for a gathering of Sorcerers and Medicine Men who deal in magic and miracles!).

We officers and a few senior NCO's were ordered to attend a pow-wow when the Commanding Officer would outline details of our part in the forthcoming Big Push – 10 a.m. in the Briqueterie, an excellent place, disused for years, far enough from the village to ensure privacy.

Watson had decribed our new CO as a good chap, who'd been in India since the war began so didn't know much of trench warfare. The old brickworks with its low cliffs sheltering from the wind made a good theatre and when I arrived the CO had taken the stage. He was sitting atop a stack of discarded bricks (probably cracked and half-baked ones). The Adjutant was handing round our copies of 'Trench Map (part of sheet 28)'. As soon as we all had a copy the CO, a tall thin man, climbed awkwardly up the brick stack to the very top and stood looking down on us.

'This pow-wow is very strictly secret,' he announced. 'In a few days we go over the top in an attack which will end the war.'

He didn't know that the Big Push ('ours or theirs') had been a sardonic joke with us for many months. He was disconcerted by some laughter; but quickly went on to claim that *this* attack was unlike previous attempts, never before had there been such careful planning. Every man in the battalion had rehearsed his individual part on model trenches of the exact size and shape to be attacked. But more important than any rehearsal, the strategy and tactics were new. He told us the official military textbooks had for a long time stated that 85 per cent of all casualties were inflicted by small-arms, not by artillery or hand-to-hand combats; this was now known to be wrong, nine out of ten casualties came from artillery fire. (I recalled Hardy's outbursts; didn't he say it is the gunners who kill, that bayonet fighting was very rare, causing less than 5 per cent of casualties?) The CO told us that under the new plan infantry would not join in the battle until after an artillery barrage had annihilated the enemy infantry. I interrupted to ask how we should know when to come in. He explained our watches would be synchronised with RA time. We were to remain in our front trench, Image Crescent, till the barrage had blasted our first objective, Jehovah: only then were we to go over the top, not to charge at the double across No-Man's-Land as in the old tactics but to walk at a steady pace towards Jehovah till our watches told us the barrage was lifting to our second objective, Jordan. Then, and not till then, we were to charge on whatever might be left of Jehovah. In spite of hints I'd picked up from Watson I was astonished to learn these details.

'Did you say *walk* across No-Man's-Land, sir?'

'Yes,' the CO replied, speaking casually as if the idea was not at all unusual. I glanced round to see what my companions made of this; all looked as blank as I daresay I had at school when confronted for the first time with an Algebra book.

'Are you serious, sir?' demanded the Captain commanding

B Company. 'You mean walk at an ordinary normal pace?'

'I am telling you . . . this show is different . . . new tactics,' replied the CO with exaggerated emphasis. Then he switched to other details. 'We don't want prisoners, disarm them and leave them for someone else to round up; consolidate gains at once and be sure men don't stop to help wounded pals. When we've taken our second objective, Jordan, consolidate quickly in case of a counter-attack. Men of the Border Regiment will carry on the attack to Jericho.'

I glanced at the map before making an obvious comment, 'We take Jehovah and Jordan and the Borders take Jericho, an advance of not much more than a thousand yards, sir. You spoke of ending the war – it's a long way from Jericho to Berlin.'

The CO standing erect on his stack of bricks, raised one hand high above his head like a clergyman about to pronounce the Benediction. In a loud voice he uttered one word, 'Cavalry'. I'd almost forgotten the word. Occasionally rumours spoke of thousands of cavalry soldiers with their horses somewhere in France, out here since 1914. The CO confirmed this – cavalry waiting for a chance to break through the rampart of trenches, will force a way to turn the enemy flanks, right and left, cutting supplies to the whole Bosche army, forcing Germany to unconditional surrender. 'It's we who will give the Cavalry the chance they've longed for,' he concluded. Daydreams fit only for Mess discussions but our Colonel believed it. He said boisterously, 'We'll all be home by Christmas,' adding as an aside, 'most of us, anyway.'

It wasn't quite the end of the pow-wow. The Captain of B Company again spoke, 'Our chaps won't take kindly to this idea of *walking* across No-Man's-Land, sir.' 'Up to you to persuade them,' said the CO, 'tell them the artillery barrage will have destroyed all enemy machine guns and mortars, there won't be any real resistance.' Then he made a joke, having

glanced at the Adjutant to be sure it was well received: 'For us
. . . this attack will be literally a walkover.'

On reflection I wondered if the Colonel had been a little
theatrical at his pow-wow. Or was it that all of us at the Front
were acting in a tragedy that could be endured only by everlasting pretence? The date was announced – over the top on the
28th. But Watson told me heavy rain had caused floods holding
up transport. There would have to be postponement till the
30th. Then the date was again changed – to the 31st. The 31st
July was my younger sister's birthday, a family anniversary,
sort of Fête Day, but for me the other sort of Fate, whatever
happens in the Big Push something of unusual significance will
happen to me: that's what war does to a man, overlays rational
expectations with superstition.

As ordered by the CO, I did my best to persuade my men
that our walk-over from Image Crescent to Jehovah would be
quite different from any previous attack; all the way under a
barrage from our Artillery and so on. But General Chaos told
me otherwise. In war things don't happen as planned, confusion is the order of every day.

I brought my men up to Image Crescent via Immovable
Avenue and then by a little-used track which I'd discovered to
Impartial Lane. It was quiet, even more quiet than I expected,
only a few solitary shells: the lull before the storm, I told myself,
thinking of the heavy barrage we had been promised. My men
were unusually quiet, in little mood for the lighthearted badin-
age and raillery which often lightened the dull monotony of a
long trek through muddy communication trenches. I repeated
to those near me the Colonel's joke about our attack being a
walkover, anxious to conceal my personal reservations now
mounting almost to apprehensions. One chap, a popular wit,
did his best: 'No need for wind-up, mates; brand new drill this
time, seconds out of the ring as usual but more haste less speed

... instead of running all that way across No-Man's-Land we're going to *walk* so we shan't be out o' breath when we says good day to Kaiser Bill ... hell of a long way to Berlin even walking.'

Walking across No-Man's-Land was a novel tactic; but without protection or ground cover a man is very vulnerable. On the Somme we'd been decimated by machine-gun fire and I reckoned that if only one German machine-gun at Jehovah Trench escaped the artillery barrage it could wipe out half my platoon. According to Watson our new Colonel was OK. Anyway he wouldn't have much to do when the Big Push got going, every detail being already worked out by Staff-Wallahs.

The day after the pow-wow the CO sent for me and said he was glad I was going to help put out the tape at Image Crescent. Watson had told him of my long experience. 'I'd like your opinion on another matter', he said. 'Platoon Commanders will know the exact moment when the barrage lifts from Jehovah Trench and you'll signal to your men to charge. I want Buglers to sound the Charge at that moment. What do you say to that?' Naturally I was flattered to be consulted by a Colonel and pleased to hear of Watson's eulogy; but how does a subaltern tell his Commanding Officer that his proposal is balderdash? I suppose I looked blank for the CO went on enthusiastically, 'Nothing like a bugle call to stimulate courage when it's most needed.'

I could only regard the man with bewildered wonder. How long had he been in trenches? Three weeks or a month since he came out? Hadn't he yet discovered that the PBI don't use bugles? My mind giggled at the thought of *Lights-Out* after evening Stand-to, *Come to the Cookhouse Door Boys* whenever the ration party arrived. 'I've got it all planned,' the CO said, 'and with something for you to do, but first I'd like your opinion of the general idea.'

I couldn't say so but thought the whole thing baloney, the dream of a senile Dug-Out. I answered the awkward question by asking another, 'How long since the bugle call Charge was used in war, sir?'

'God knows; but a great tradition.'

Bows and arrows a great tradition too, I thought, but why waste time talking? Surely this barmy idea was dead already. 'There are no buglers or bugles at the Front, sir.'

He wasn't abashed. 'That's where you come in,' he said, as if asking a medicine man to perform a miracle. He elaborated. I was to find eight men in the battalion who were trained buglers before they came out. The Quartermaster would get instruments for them, probably from the Rouen Base.

'Not much time for the men you pick to practise,' said the CO. 'You'll have to keep them at it. They'll know the common calls but may not remember The Charge. Make certain they get it right.'

I had other preparations before the attack, like going up to Image Crescent with Watson to reconnoitre, so I was reluctant to become involved in this fantasy. I seized on the chance to get clear of it, 'Sorry, sir, but I don't *know* The Charge. Couldn't tell if they sounded it or were playing odd notes from *Keep the Home Fires Burning*.' But the CO argued as though determined to convince me without giving an order which I must obey. He pointed out that in a crisis men tend to be unduly aware of themselves, feel isolated, and a bugle call assures them they are not acting alone, that others are called to act with them. I'd experienced that isolation feeling myself more than once and was impressed. Rather weakly I said I'd do my best to find a few men who could play and perhaps one or two might know The Charge. The CO actually thanked me, adding there was a further problem he would have to overcome – buglers must be armed, but not with rifle or bayonet. Next day he told me with great satisfaction that he'd arranged each bugler should be armed with an officer's pistol, there were enough in QM's stores. And then, as though doing me a favour, added, 'I want you to show them how to use the weapon, take them somewhere and give them a little practice.'

When I told Watson he laughed, 'Playing at war, Glory-War. Might as well send officers over the top with drawn swords.'

One afternoon I took ten buglers to the Etang de Zoote, a pond remote from Civilians, where they could practise shooting at floating bottles. I told them to stand in line, fire in turn one at a time and always wait till they saw the splash of the last man's shot. My efforts at control didn't match their excitement. Several waved their pistols over their heads in imitation of American film stars, one almost shot his neighbour, another put a bullet into the ground just short of his own foot. When I'd been twice narrowly missed I said, 'Enough. When the time comes remember you've a better weapon than any Jerry.'

As Watson said, we had been told that behind us was going to be the biggest concentration of guns ever: all the buglers in the British army massed together and blowing their heads off wouldn't be heard by anyone.

Watson and I waited till the moon was down before putting out the direction tape in No-Man's-Land, an easier job than we had expected. Unluckily I tripped and fell full length into a disused sap full of stinking stagnant water. When I got back to Image Crescent soaked to the skin and shivering, my splendid old-soldier batman Tidmarsh looked at me with reproach, rather as my mother used to when I came home with muddy clothes from fishing in a burn on Blackford Hill, but he said nothing. Tidmarsh had been my batman for months. We were not exactly friends because of the differences of social class.

but, accepting these differences, we were not separated by them. Each regarded the other as a personality to be respected. Tidmarsh had never been to school, just picked up reading and writing. I told him once how thrilled I'd been at Toc H to see their slogan, 'All rank abandon ye who enter here', explaining, rather sententiously, it was a deliberate misquotation from Dante. Tidmarsh said, 'Must have rank in the army, sir, to establish authority, but rank does not give anyone superiority of character.' Obviously perhaps, but typical of his wise remarks, some of which have remained with me through life.

My watch told me it was past midnight, the hands moving inexorably into 31st July. Normally the hour or so before dawn is occupied with what might be called trench housekeeping – sorting and storing what the ration party has brought up, re-stocking ammunition, minor repairs to dug-outs, and so on. This night we had no such tasks to distract us: shortly we should leave Image Crescent for ever, our next quarters Jehovah or Jordan. The men stood about in twos and threes waiting, nothing to do, listless, for the most part silent. I knew and shared their common thought – that half of us would be dead before the first glint of sun peeped over the horizon. What can men talk about, knowing what all are thinking? I walked up and down along the trench wanting to show insensibility, knowing I was watched by all. To my surprise Tidmarsh appeared with a mug of steaming hot tea. 'How the devil did you manage this?' I asked, 'It'll save my life.' (How clichés mock us!) One mug for so many, I the privileged one. Tidmarsh said for all to hear, 'You're shivering with cold, sir, more than any of us.' He raised a little laugh by sniffing at my drenched uniform. 'Can't say I like the French perfume you use, sir.' Someone asked, 'Smell any rum, Tid?' But the old joke about a rum ration which ends up in the Sergeant's Mess seemed stale.

Some of my men had been out only a few weeks. I hardly recognised them in the quarter light of a summer dawn. With thirty-five minutes to go I decided I must walk the whole length of Image Crescent stopping a moment to exchange a few words with every man, or if no words came, at least swap a look. A look? What could a look say? Perhaps only – 'You or me?' or 'Will it be both of us?' Not really morbid – reality.

Whenever possible we turned from war to sport so I attempted a little light conversation, 'After we've settled this show, we'll play the final of our Inter-Company . . . That was a great save by Corporal Budge in the match against B Company . . . Pity no handicaps in footer, the RSM weighs 17 stone, no fun being charged by him.' Heavy going, like an awkward farewell at a railway station waiting for the guard's whistle and the train to start.

A few men I knew very well, recalling intimacies of their private lives from letters I'd censored. I wondered at times if they realised, as they wrote, that I was the censor – such intimacies!

I stood before a man I'd taken with me on patrol, a good chap in a tight place, and I remembered what he'd written to his wife – 'I'm due for leave soon. If I find you've been carrying on with that Wade fellow I'll bash his face in and give you a belting you'll never forget.' The odds were he'd never go on leave.

Another man, rather old for trenches, about thirty I thought, exchanged with me a thoughtful look while I recalled an angry letter telling his wife that when the war ended and he came home, she'd have to send her mother packing, 'no room in our home for the old bitch.' Perhaps that problem too would be solved within the hour.

Once I felt embarrassed; yes, actually embarrassed, even in these fleeting moments. I was standing before a chap about my own age, strong vigorous man who played outside-left for the

Company. Better educated than most. Gave me a look which seemed to have appeal in it as though I, an officer, might control events. In a recent batch of letters was one from him to a girl which I didn't quite understand, but am not likely to forget: 'Reckon I'll be in next lot for leave. When I get home you know what I want from you.' He used a word I didn't properly understand, but I suppose she did. The conclusion was definite, 'that's what I am going to do with you, my girl, and you're going to like it; anyway, you'll have to take it lying down.' I'd been shocked reading that letter, now it seemed different. I hoped he would survive this morning and get what he wanted, and have a lot of children and grandchildren.

With nine minutes in hand I remembered last warnings. Getting together little groups I told them, 'Two final warnings, whatever happens you've got to keep going to the final objective, Jordan. No prisoners. If a Jerry with hands up cries *kamerad*, disarm him and boot him across No-Man's-Land in this direction. Still more important, don't stop to help any of our wounded, stretcher-bearers do that.'

'Not always stretcher-bearers around when they're wanted,' said a man who'd been with me on the Somme.

'Our job is to fight. To falter for any purpose whatever is a serious crime. Field Service Pocket Book, (under Court-Martial) gives the punishment as up to ten years hard labour in a civil prison.'

'Cheap at the price, sir,' he said with a laugh, 'Ten years in the Scrubs, starting right now, 'ud do me a proper treat.'

Total silence commanded the last two minutes, silence like in an empty dark cathedral. The Bosche too were silent; they might have been asleep. I thought of the Colonel's assurance that the artillery barrage, an umbrella beneath which we were to walk, would be of unprecedented strength. The hands of my watch moved through the last five seconds, then a single gun somewhere about Verbrandenmolen opened fire, a very small gun to my expectant ears, almost apologetic like a shy boy entering a fashionable party.

An immense number of guns of all types and sizes answered the Verbrandenmolen signal, the greatest volume of gunfire ever heard. The daylight was still feeble at 3.05 a.m., as though a lazy Dawn, turning over in bed, muttered, 'just a minute or two longer'. We, starting the Big Push, had no option, time for us (conventional time now) was inexorable, we were part of a programme. The light would grow stronger while we got up, scrambling from Image Crescent to walk across No-Man's-Land, but it looked like being a dull morning.

The vast noise filled me with awe (that blend of holy wonder and personal abasement) reminding me of what someone called 'the blind fury of Creation'. The earth reeled and rocked as when God threw up ranges of high Alps and shifted Continents hither and thither. Anxious doubts during the time of waiting dissolved, my spirits rebounded to ecstasy, outside myself.

I spaced my men along the tape evenly, one metre or so apart. Shells from our barrage screeched just over our heads. The enemy artillery, taken by surprise, had not yet opened fire. I set a steady walking pace, everything going according to plan. But after a few steps I found myself in a huddle on the ground, gasping for breath, bewildered. The blast of a shell had thrown me down violently. As I struggled to get up, to regain balance, still confused, I realised that what seemed to be an unrecognisable heap on the ground alongside me was, in fact, a man; one arm extended, a long bare arm disclaiming any connection with the body, the hand open with fingers wide apart as though glad to be done with grasping. Undoubtedly a Goner. I'd seen many such empty bodies with that general appearance of having been thrown away in a hurry, no longer wanted. When I regained my balance and my composure, I saw several gaps in our line: casualties. Could only be from a 'short-fall', one of our own shells, what the Artillery called 'short rounds'. I'd never worried about 'short-falls' before, they landed in the open when we were below ground in trenches, but it was bad luck to have one at the very start of our walk-over attack. Almost at once we had another . . . shrapnel . . . bursting low. Notwithstanding the solid noise of the barrage, I could pick out the zip-zip of metal fragments whizzing past my ears. A third 'short-fall' killed my sergeant and two men. The situation was serious. We were about halfway to Jehovah and a third of our strength already casualties. The mind works so much faster than the body acts. I found my thoughts debating why so many short-falls: can it be that a big concentration of guns on a short front also concentrates the short-falls? Surely that would have been foreseen by whoever planned this battle? No time for theories, the light was now strong enough to see what damage our gunners had done to Jehovah. I glanced at my watch. In a few moments we must make our charge at the double.

My reflections were cut short. From the battered parapet of Jehovah, a little to my left, I saw the flash of a rifle: so we could expect some resistance. Another rifle flash, this one straight in front . . . a knock-out blow . . . legs sagging . . . collapse: and as I crossed the hazy limits of consciousness into the non-world, I knew I had been shot through the head.

*   *   *

> How long in that same fit I lay,
> I have not to declare:
> But ere my living life return'd,
> I heard, and in my soul discerned
> Two voices in the air.

I hope it's not presumption for an Ancient Warrior to borrow a few words of immortal poetry. Coleridge's Mariner was telling a story with a moral; my fragment of autobiography has no moral and is merely an account of war as experienced by one common-or-garden infantry subaltern. But my last experience was so fantastic that the facts can do with a hint of poetry to help them snuggle down alongside Truth.

I saw a rifle fired point-blank in my direction as I was walking towards Jehovah trench, felt a knock-out blow, knew I'd been hit in the head, that my legs were giving way, my body collapsing, my mind surrendering consciousness. These facts were registered in less time than they take to tell, but it's not sufficient merely to say, 'I was there and I saw it.' Between dawn and dusk on the 31st July, 1917 I was sometimes *not* there. How long I lay in the first fit of total unconsciousness I do not know. Thereafter, I drifted in and out of varied degrees of consciousness; sometimes eyes closed, my mind wayward as in a dream, at other times wide-eyed and as clear-thinking as I've ever been. Such was my last experience of war, 'a mighty sum of things forever speaking', in my memory.

No sensation of having a body, no feeling in torso or limbs. No pain, of course; the dead don't feel.

Drowsy contentment, a faint sound as of distant thunder . . . war now moved on . . . Time doesn't exist any more . . . all used up, come to an end . . . there would be no more Time . . . just blank eternity.

Perfect content . . . not a single worry . . . war far away . . . not *my* war now . . . not my responsibility . . . doesn't matter how the battle's going . . . or when the war will end . . . doesn't matter . . . nothing matters, not even who wins the war . . . can't concern the dead . . . when you're dead all that commotion of war has no meaning . . . dies with you . . . in truth all

over and done with before the Generals start to write their
histories.

Is unconsciousness the same as sleep? Anyway I wallow in
the bliss of unresponsibility, now extended from war to life. A
living man cannot escape responsibilities imposed on him
through life, as long as he lives, even to an old man's chair. For
me all responsibilities are ended . . . Life can't hang a single
duty round my neck now. I am nothing . . . Oh! the bliss of not
being.

A sound outside my mind stirred me to fresh awareness – two
voices in the air. I opened my eyes (astonished to discover that
my eyes had not been shot away). I lay on the rim of a shell hole.
Two men, at a lower level, were staring up at me, on the
ground between them a stretcher. Of course – stretcher-
bearers, gleaning the battlefield, collecting wounded who'd
been overlooked in the first harvest. Strong men, tough chaps,
accustomed to horror-sights, to mutilations and handling the
half-dead. No use for me. I wasn't worth gleaning. I wanted to
shoo them away, to shout, 'For God's sake go away, my
number's up and I'm content', but I could not speak, or make
any sound, or so much as raise a warning hand. I was as
helpless as any decaying corpse on any battlefield. But I could
hear, my ears still worked.

'Poor bugger looks like he's a Goner.'

'Saw his eyes flicker.'

'Waste o' time I reckon. Take off his waterbottle, put it where
'e can reach it if 'e wants a drink.'

''Ow the 'ell could 'e drink with that face? You lookin' for a
bloody miracle?'

'No, he's a Goner, for sure. Waste o' time. Customer for us over there, on the wire, see – moving 'is arm. Come on.'

They took up their stretcher and went . . . to my relief. Contentment restored me to the bliss of unconsciousness. Maybe I slept. Even dying men sleep, and in trenches you get hungry for sleep.

Maybe it was several hours of sleep from which I awoke. Certainly I was more perceptive. I remembered the stretcher-bearers. I opened my eyes again. Nothing to see, and all around a solemn stillness holds.

> So lonely 'twas that God himself
> Scarce seemed there to be.

I noticed in my shell hole bits and pieces of rubble in the churned earth and stones, rubble from some destroyed building – Graveyard Cottage presumably, the only feature between Image Crescent and Jehovah on sheet 28 of Trench Map, printed in Southampton, April 1917. Graveyard Cottage, an English translation from French no doubt; but certainly not my invented name. Not that the cottage existed, any more than I did. Must have been a cemetery here once: not only was my number up . . . I was already in a burial gound.

'Blessed are those who mourn, for they shall be comforted'. I was haunted by the look of everlasting sadness in my mother's face when I was on leave . . . My parents would now receive that telegram, 'died of wounds', same as my brother. And my sisters: of course, the younger one's birthday today, 31st July, that deep but illogical feeling that it would be a fateful day for me! But now I knew, beyond all superstitious credulity, that in Death there is no grief. Those who mourn here cannot take grief with them when they die, any more than a millionaire can take his money; the edge of sorrow is blunted here on earth.'

Dying people recall the whole of their life in a series of mental pictures, so it is said. My twenty years came as a continuous story, like in a moving-picture film at a cinema. And trivial matters of which I had been ashamed came foremost, things I had tried to forget – petty deceits at home, lies at school, panic fears like that first 'Little Willie' shell at Poperinghe, and people I'd been too busy to help. Shameful things brought now to light, already dead, dismissed, written off, the slate clean.

> Is it the all severest mode
> To see ourselves with the eyes of God?
> God rather grant at his assize
> He sees us not with our own eyes.

As such patches of consecutive thought returned I felt free as I'd never been free in Life. Already well on the way to I-don't-know-where, I was beyond Fear, Danger, Grief.

Awakening came, a rough awakening – to reality. My body hadn't moved on the ground where it had been from a little after 3 a.m. till mid-afternoon, hadn't moved an inch in any direction, must have looked as solidly dead as a dummy in a shop window displaying ready-made clothes. Suddenly the ground beneath me shuddered as in an earthquake, followed instantly by the sound of a detonating shell – and I knew the shell to be one from the new Wipers Express. What's more, I understood exactly the significance – Wipers Express shells falling around where our attack began would harass reinforcements and Graveyard Cottage gave enemy gunners a measured-by-map target. The Bosche would keep it up, a shell every few minutes. So this awakening, with imagination built on experience, showed me what to expect, and in that way brought me right back into the war. No question of surviving, my life was ebbing fast; there could be no turn of *that* tide, nor did I have any sense of responsibility or purpose.

165

Was I afraid of Wipers Express shells? I am not sure. My recollection of what happened is confused. With awakened consciousness came pain, pain in my head, at first a steady dull sensation making concentration of thought or purpose difficult. All the same I was spurred to action: I was warm, my clothes dry, but the sun would set and a night of exposure finish me off unpleasantly, not in calm content. A second Wipers Express might give me another wound, increasing the pain to be endured. I tried to crawl away from Graveyard Cottage, limbs stiff, headache becoming a sharp agony. I fainted but later tried again. Increasing pain suggested I'd do better to stand rather than go on all fours with head bent. I tried and tried again, always overcome by dizziness; but I was determined to stand upright, shells or no shells, and somehow stagger across the wasteland of our battlefield. Confused as I was, I shan't forget the moment of excitement when I saw a man's head above what the barrage had left of our first objective, Jehovah trench, near where it joined Illusive trench.

I made an effort to keep standing till I was seen. A voice said, 'Gorblimey, that bugger didn't 'arf cop it.' Strong arms took mine, led me in short steps somewhere . . . flat on a stretcher . . . a glimpse from an ambulance window of the ruins of the Cloth Hall . . . mild indignation . . . I could have shown them a safer route avoiding Ypres. At last, clear of that stricken town I knew I was on the road to Vlamertinghe, beyond even the range of a Wipers Express. Somewhere before dark my stretcher was on flat ground in a field full of stretchers, seemingly acres of stretchers, as though we were a carefully cultivated crop of some choice plant ready for harvest, waiting to be reaped. My heart leaped up when I beheld an English girl kneeling beside me, gentle hands seeking where to give me an injection – then back to unconsciousness. Next, I was looking from the window of a stationary hospital train, recognising the harbour of

Boulogne. Two days, I think, in a bed, a real bed, in the Casino – this time indignant to discover my legs still caked with Flanders mud. Don't they wash patients in hospital? Probably I was under sedation because I next remember being aboard a hospital ship, SS *St Denis*, in the harbour awaiting nightfall, before crossing the English Channel. I lay in a stretcher very contented while all the wounded around me sang softly, the most popular song of the PBI, *There's a long long trail a'winding into the land of my dreams.*

CHAPTER ELEVEN

Infinite Vexation

As I sat by the fire in an old man's chair concluding this fragment of a twentieth-century life story, my mind toyed with words from a sixteenth-century play:

> I am i' th' way to study a long silence:
> To prate were idle . . .
> There's nothing of so infinite vexation
> As man's own thoughts.
>
> I have caught
> An everlasting cold; I have lost my voice
> Most irrecoverably.

Some vexation of thought was to be expected. My experiences of war ended with that sedative of song-singing aboard the hospital ship, *St Denis*, by men with whom I had shared dangers and hardships. A few days later, back in England, I made a blank restart of life. At first I was no better than an intelligent animal, incapable of consecutive thought. Words spoken by the doctor to the ward sister, casual remarks of my nurse, and the way my wounds were dressed, revealed to me gradually that I had not been wounded by a rifle shot fired from Jehovah trench, but by a part or parts of a shell – as like as not a short-fall of our own artillery. Whatever penetrated my head entered the upper part of the right cheek, fractured the jaw and the septum of the nose and did considerable damage to the mouth before passing out through a large hole in the left cheek.

I had lost my voice most irrecoverably. My nurse thoughtfully brought me a pad and pencil, and also a printed card with such phrases as 'have been wounded . . . in hospital at . . . will write soon.' She said, 'Difficult to write when you're flat on your back and can't move your head but see if you can address this card to your parents; they'll be anxious.' I scrawled on the pad, 'Where am I?' She laughed, amused by this mode of communication between us, 'This is the Royal Herbert Hospital, London. Proper spit-and-polish army outfit I can tell you! But you needn't write that on the card!'

Silly girl, I thought (though, of course, I was already madly in love with her). Whoever heard of a *Royal* Herbert? Must be Albert, Royal Albert, King of the Belgians, the little country Germany invaded which started the war. So in due course this card brought my worried mother from Edinburgh to London where she spent two days seeking an Albert Hospital.

With sleepy mind and half-closed eyes I watched my mother. Several times I'd woken to see her sitting patiently at my bedside as though content to just soak in the fact of my existence. We could not talk even when my bemused mind was momentarily clear and, to be sure, my thoughts were generally confused; if not of infinite vexation, then from lassitude (perhaps in part caused by narcotic drugs) and bouts of exhaustion after the agonising pain every time my wounds were dressed. Lazily I watched her moving lips, perhaps in part lip-read, for the dumb like the deaf become quick-eyed. I heard what she said, realised she was talking with my doctor, and rather to my surprise I cottoned on to the general drift of their remarks.

He was reporting on my condition: 'Remarkable progress . . . soon have him sitting up . . . feeding cup a few weeks longer till he can feed himself. . . no solid food for several months.' She asked a question which I didn't catch. He gave himself time for a considered reply. 'Not much permanent disability; he'll be able to make himself understood by you and your family in general conversation.'

So that was my future – in the way to study a long silence, but not the silence of death which the playwright meant. At Graveyard Cottage I was convinced I was dying. Now, in hospital, I began to think of life as probable. I was disinclined to remember the past or consider any future. I suppose I more or less accepted a life with some degree of disability, and I knew beyond any doubt I should never be fit to fight again. Recovery would be long but I was only twenty, still two score years and ten.

My mother, holding her head high, spoke slowly and with reverence, 'Doctor, I know you will do everything possible for my son. I thank you. I thank God my boy is alive, and I thank God his wounds are so bad he will never again know war.' A simple and sincere little speech, but I wondered how the doctor would take it. In childhood, at home and in church, we were taught to consider the word God as sacred, not to be used cheaply. In the army and the wider world, 'God' was merely an ejaculation – God knows! Good God! God forbid! I avoided such casual use. I was a little sensitive over my mother's piety, rather as a boy on school speech day fears his mother may turn up extravagantly dressed. She who had been the life and soul of our childhood delights was now overdrawn at the Bank of Joy, in credit only with the Bank of Piety. Was the doctor amused by her thanking God so devoutly? Was he hiding a smile? I couldn't twist my head round enough to see his face, but I need not have worried. There was a pause before he spoke, then what he said was in a low voice, perhaps not wishing to be overheard.

'I am told you lost a son early in the war. After long anxiety you have reason to thank God for what has happened to this boy. Madam, I envy you. My profession is dedicated to restoring health where it has been lost, healing the sick, relieving suffering. A Latin tag often quoted in my profession says, 'the best remedy for injuries is to forget them'. Sound advice, but not easy for the severely wounded, and war wounds are in the mind as well as in the body. Alas! my duty in war is to practise my medical knowledge so that patients can be sent back to the front as soon as possible. For you the war is over, all my skill won't patch up your son to A1 standard. For me the war goes on. My successes, so rewarding in peace-time, often send men back to that existence of violence and destruction. Madam, I envy you that you have reason to thank God. I have no reason to do so.'

At the Front I carried with me everywhere, day and night, in pack or pocket, my most cherished possession, *The Golden Treasury*. I still have the book, with the pencil markings I made in trenches. Sixteen of the marked passages are in poems by Browning, so it's not surprising that a line from this poet haunted me during the days and weeks and months I was in hospital with nothing to do but think, and think for myself, no one telling me what to think, 'This life must be lived out and a grave thoroughly earned.' That was the future to be faced. Fifteen months in trenches and going 'over the top' disillusioned me, changed me, left marks deeper than the scars on my face. Disillusion is not an emotional reaction. It is change coming from undisturbed thinking about experienced reality. My future does not belong to anyone else. I, and I alone, can use my life, can act as if what I do makes a difference.

After months in hospitals I was examined by a Medical Board of three doctors – their verdict, 'Twenty per cent permanent disability, unfit for further service abroad.' I had supposed my general recovery to be good. I was mobile and my speech was now quite intelligible, so this judgement came as rather a shock. My fighting days were over. American troops now arriving in the trenches must eventually bring victory. I saw in my mind's eye an apparently endless succession of these American young men born in Europe (or the sons of earlier emigrants) now returning from the New World to take part in the Great War in Europe. The war would go on without me.

About eight months before Armistice Day, November 1918, the War Office issued a memorandum, *Training for Disabled Officers before returning to Civil Life*. More bumf, I thought: but the interview I then had with a Staff Officer began with a very practical question, 'Before we decide on your training, Old Man, have you any pre-war commitments, any employer keeping open a job for you?' I recalled plans made when I was in the sixth form at school. I'd passed Edinburgh University entrance exam for medical students and the London Missionary Society (connected with our church) promised help with fees on the understanding that when qualified I'd go as a medical missionary to China.

Somewhere I'd read a comment, 'War is the forcing-house of character,' an evocative phrase. Army doctors were concerned only with my physical condition, but had I been wounded mentally? What of my outlook on Life and the world about me? In short were my moral judgements twenty per cent disabled . . . and permanently? After more than a year in trenches I was a different person. I now knew with absolute conviction that my schoolboy idealism was dead, stone dead, killed in the forcing-house of character. I could never be a missionary and my thoughts galloped on without pausing to ask why.

'You seem uncertain,' observed the Staff Officer. 'What were you doing pre-war?'

'At school,' I replied. 'I hadn't exactly any commitments, only plans which are a wash-out now.'

'That makes our job easy. We can start training you for anything you fancy.' He added with a laugh, 'All the world before you, Old Man.'

I was glad my war was over but I felt some satisfaction in that I had acquired an experience. I even felt a little pity for chaps in the next generation who must face a lifetime without first-hand knowledge of war. Of course, the horror and ugliness could never be cleansed, would be part of me forever, and some beliefs of my childhood had been shaken, especially by my outspoken friend, Hardy. The Toc H slogan, 'All rank abandon ye who enter here,' had become for me, 'Abandon dogmas ye who follow Christ'.

Although I was still in the army my training for civilian life cut me off from army contacts. I mixed more and more with civilians and by the summer of 1918 many of them anticipated peace; eager to get back to the good old times, the end of rations and shortages, hang the Kaiser, make Germany pay the astronomical costs of the war, and so on. No civilians seemed to have any conception of the nature of war, what war is like in practice, the inevitable changes it brings. I knew it was too soon for me to make final judgements and that when I was fully trained to civilian life I might look upon war rather differently; but what astonished me was to hear occasionally talk of our war as a world war – which, of course it wasn't. It may have been caused by politics, diplomacy, economics, and its after-effects may be worldwide, but war was fighting, only fighting, nothing else; and we PBI who did the fighting knew that our war was (with trivial exceptions) European. It was started in Europe by European nations fighting one another, with European soldiers and European weapons, and all of us claiming that God was in it too, fighting on our side. As I recalled my experiences I didn't forget those coloured soldiers on parade at Rouen. I'd never seen them, or any coloured men, in trenches or anywhere near the Front. An officer from our second battalion in India had explained to

173

me that 'native' soldiers (as he called them) were token troops, conscripted, trained and officered by Europeans, not at all representative of the big nations from which they came.

The Great War (as it was correctly named) was not a World War. The majority of Mankind stood aside from it: millions of spectators, who doubtless watched in wonder to see the all-powerful Christian white men slaughtering one another in barbarous ways. My thoughts, becoming centered by reflections on this misnomer, suddenly saw why I could not go to China as a missionary.